D1173435

Free to Stay at Home

Free to Stay at Home

A Woman's Alternative

Marilee Horton

A Special Edition for "Focus on the Family"
published by

WORD BOOKS
PUBLISHER
WACO, TEXAS

A DIVISION OF
WORD, INCORPORATED

All Scripture quotations are from the King James Version of the Bible, unless otherwise identified, as follows: AB, from *The Amplified Bible*, copyright © 1958 by the Lockman Foundation; RSV, from The Revised Standard Version of the Bible, copyright 1946, 1952, © 1971, 1973 by The Division of Christian Education of The National Council of The Churches of Christ in the U.S.A., and used by permission.

Grateful acknowledgment is made to the following for their permission to use selected passages from their publications: Baker Book House, from *The Unwanted Generation* by Paul D. Meier and Linda Burnett, copyright 1980 Baker Book House and used by permission; Harvest House Publishers, from *The Spirit Controlled Woman* by Beverly LaHaye, copyright 1976 Harvest House Publishers, 1075 Arrowsmith, Eugene, Oregon 97402; Moody Press, from *Love, Honor—and Be Free* by Maxine Hancock, copyright 1975 Moody Press, Moody Bible Institute of Chicago, used by permission; Lynda G. Parry, from her article "Why Working Mothers Make Me Mad," published in *McCall's*, February 1981; Rawson, Wade Publishers, Inc., from *The Two-Paycheck Marriage* by Caroline Bird, copyright © 1979, Caroline Bird, reprinted with the permission of Rawson, Wade Publishers, Inc.; Fleming H. Revell Company, from *I Am a Woman by God's Design* by Beverly LaHaye, copyright © 1980 by Beverly LaHaye, from *Hear the Children Crying* by Dale Evans Rogers with Frank S. Mead, copyright © 1978 by Dale Evans Rogers, and from *What Is a Family?* by Edith Schaeffer, copyright © 1975 by Edith Schaeffer, published by Fleming H. Revell Company, used by permission; Tyndale House Publishers, Inc., from *Let Me Be a Woman* by Elisabeth Elliott © 1976 and from *What Wives Wish Their Husbands Knew about Women* by Dr. James Dobson, © 1975, Published by Tyndale House Publishers, Inc., used by permission; Zondervan Publishing House, from *The Act of Marriage* by Tim and Beverly LaHaye, copyright © 1976 by The Zondervan Corporation, and from *How to Really Love Your Wife* by Dean Merrill, previously titled *The Husband Book*, copyright © 1977 by The Zondervan Corporation, used by permission.

ISBN 0-8499-2969-5
Library of Congress catalog card number: 82–050511

Printed in the United States of America

Contents

Preface

*T*here was no way of knowing that *Free to Stay at Home* was being conceived that day fifteen years ago when I rather woefully walked into my handsome office in Montgomery, Alabama, and resigned an executive secretarial position that I adored. The reasons for that very personal decision, made with great reservations, might still be locked within my heart if it had not been for questions I was asked at a women's retreat: Why did I resign the beginnings of a career (I didn't plan always to be a secretary)? What were the end results? Had I made the right choice? Was it worth it to me? To my family?

At the end of the long line of women who had stayed to speak with me after my talk was a young, blond mother of three. She summed up what most of them were saying. "Why are we Christian women falling for all the wrong teaching? Why aren't more people giving us direction? We either seem to get no advice or the wrong kind. Why can't someone give us a guidebook?"

So *Free to Stay at Home* was born and is riding upstream, against loudly vocalized anti-housewife sentiment, on a raft made up of just two boards, Titus 2:4 and 5: "That they may teach the young women to be sober, to love their husbands, to love their children, to be discreet, chaste, keepers at home, good, obedient to their own husbands, that the word of God be not blasphemed." I am tied to that raft by Titus 2:1, "But speak thou the things which become sound doctrine."

If millions of dollars can be spent to preserve the snail darter, why are millions being spent to eliminate another endangered species—me? As I observe the energetic effort being spent on deleting the traditional role models of mother and homemaker from textbooks, TV, and movies, I am deeply hurt that so many people would consider what I do so worthless that a snail darter is more to be preserved. I know what I do and what millions of other women do in the home is vitally important. Checking the kids into day care, deli foods out of the market, time cards into slots, and husbands somewhere between the eleven o'clock news and sandman time may be what you have chosen. For many, I know, it may be a necessity. In either case, fine—I'm just asking that you not take away the dignity of the rest of us by making us feel like second-class citizens. The new ethic says, "If it feels good, do it." Please, just leave our role models alone. We feel good.

Free to Stay at Home is dedicated to the theme that the traditional female role is basic to the fabric of our society. There must be clear understanding of and a definite distinction between what is male and what is female. That doesn't mean that some women shouldn't hold positions once held solely by men, or vice versa. It just means we must preserve, as the norm, the traditional roles of mother as nurturer and father as provider-protector. Our real strength lies not in our sameness but in our diversity.

MARILEE HORTON

1. Superwoman Retires

That they may teach the young women to be . . . keepers at home . . .

Titus 2:3, 5

The brisk Alabama chill glazed our faces as we left the warmth of our car to dash into church for the Sunday evening service. Strains of "Amazing Grace" masked out our somewhat noisy family procession down the aisle to the closest available pew, where Marvin and I arranged the children between us to discourage the usual pinching and whispering. I tried to catch my breath, relax and shut out the cares of everyday life and slip into the "spiritual" part of my week. A brand, spanking new Christian of only a few months, I hadn't yet learned that you don't slip in and out of spirituality. I *had* learned that the outward me slipped back into the old stale ways oftener than I cared to remember, and I needed the renewed strength these services always gave me.

So I listened with anticipation as our pastor explained to us that we would be leaving a study of the doctrine of redemption and beginning a study on Biblical conduct for the Christian family.

The text for the service was from chapter 2 of Titus. I was, as usual, busy marking verses with my red pen while the pastor read. The passage spoke about men and women who were older, not necessarily in years but older in the Lord, how their lives should be "sober, grave, temperate, sound in faith, in charity, in pa-

9

tience . . . not false accusers, not given to much wine, teachers of good things." My heart was saying *amen* to all that I was hearing. The pastor emphasized that the older women were to teach younger women "to be sober, to love their husbands, to love their children, to be discreet, chaste, keepers at home, obedient to their own husbands, that the word of God be not blasphemed."

My pen froze under the words *keepers at home.* At first I wondered what it meant, but somehow, deep in my soul I knew. The pastor was reading on, but my mind wouldn't proceed. All I could hear was "keepers at home, keepers at home, KEEPERS AT HOME!"

I don't remember anything else about that service except that I was strangely disturbed when we got home. Not comforted and encouraged and cheered as usual, but agitated, and I didn't understand why. That phrase *keepers at home* seemed to be slapping me in the face over and over again.

I momentarily brushed aside the sensation while praying with the children. We prayed for Mark's temper, that he wouldn't fight at school and that Mandi would have her fears of *everything* relieved, and that Mike would get up quickly in the morning and be in a better mood so that I could get to work on time with a minimum of frustration. Amen!

After dealing with the children's extreme bedtime thirst and the inevitable shrinking bladders that demanded immediate attention and the extra kisses that of course can't be denied, I finally left their rooms—weary.

I heated apple cider for Marvin and me to drink in front of the fireplace. As he stirred the fire with a poker, I asked, "Honey, what do you think Pastor meant about that message on 'Keepers at Home'?"

He looked puzzled. "I must have missed something. What do *you* think he meant?"

"Surely he didn't mean that I should quit my job and just stay home. We both know how badly we need the money ever since we lost so much on that insurance stock."

"Honey, if you want to quit work," he said, smiling, "we can manage somehow."

I was irritated at his optimism. "I *don't want* to quit. This is the best job I have ever had. I have a good sitter with the children, and you know I have lots of energy—I keep up the house and serve good meals and all the rest. I could give Superwoman a good race!"

Yawning widely, he stretched. Then he crossed the room to where I sat in the brown wingback chair and bent to kiss me. "Superwoman, you do whatever makes you happy. Just pray about it, but don't stay up too long. I'm going on to bed."

I did stay up too long that night, wrestling with the verse that contained that phrase, "keepers at home," with the Spirit of God, and with my own intense self-fulfillment goals.

I couldn't go to bed until peace was restored. I had searched twenty-seven years for peace in every conceivable place—in material things such as homes, furniture, cars, clothes; in relationships, marriage, motherhood, friendships; in substitute peace-promisers such as alcohol and pills. I was always disappointed. I wondered, "Is this all there is?"

That was until the two months prior to this when I met the Prince of Peace. I had struggled for several months over the fact that God *could* love *me* or that He could forgive me for all my sins. Finally, at the end of the proverbial rope, I cried out to God asking Him to forgive my sins and thanking Him for loving me so much that He was willing to send His Son to die on a cross in my place. I believed that night that God accepted and approved of Christ's sacrifice on my behalf.

Peace entered my life that night. I had sought after peace so long that when this came it seemed enough. Sometime later, I realized all that I received through Christ—a new name, a new future, a new destination, a new power to live by, and all the benefits of becoming a child of God. But that night, John 14:27 was enough: "Peace I leave with you, my peace I give unto you: not as the world giveth, give I unto you. Let not your heart be troubled, neither let it be afraid."

Now, on this December night, after hearing the Titus 2 message, the peace was disturbed. Was Christianity, after all, just another crutch to get you through a bad time? Was it going to fail me, as everything else had?

In bitter tears, I grabbed my Bible. Christianity *had* to work; I had nowhere else to turn, and I was jealous for the peace I'd experienced for such a brief period. I had to have it back, no matter the cost. I turned to Titus 2 and read it over and over. No matter how hard I tried to concentrate on the other parts of the verses of the pastor's text, I was stuck on "keepers at home." Anger welled up as I tried to communicate with God.

"But Lord, staying home full time with the kids and housekeeping is not for everyone. What do you want of me?"

Keeper at Home.

"I know, Lord, the kids do seem to be getting into a lot of trouble, but I promise to try and spend more time with them. I know I've structured our family life too severely and we don't have time to work out our problems. I know that sometimes our family seems to be coming apart, but I can do better, Lord. O.K.?"

Keeper at home.

I remembered that the day before one of the neighbors had hinted that we were in for a lot of trouble with our boys as we struggled to put out a brush fire the boys had started. The neighbor indicated that the sitter didn't observe things as well as a mother might. And this same neighbor had had to call me twice at work to tell me Mark had been hurt and needed stitches, and I had had to drive forty-five minutes to get home. I felt some shame as I remembered.

I also remember how badly we needed money.

As I began to see the evidence that the problems caused by my working outweighed the advantages, I sobbed harder.

"But, Lord, I love my job. I like wearing nice clothes and leaving the cares behind for a few hours, and talking with adults. I like being stimulated mentally. And I love my newly decorated office that gets cleaned up at night. I like my boss who seems to appreciate my work. O Lord, I am afraid to stay home. What if I'm not good at it? You remember how bored I got when I quit after the boys were born. What if I get bored again?"

The more I prayed, the more I saw of my true character coming to the surface. "O God, I hate myself this way. Take away the selfishness and show me what to do."

Keeper at home.

When the sun began to come up over our home on Lawrence Street, I knew the direction I had to take.

I was exhausted as I made the rounds to wake my family. My eyes were red and swollen from crying, and I didn't want to face going to work.

After the kids were on the way to school, I went to my pastor's home. Keeping my sunglasses on, I blurted out through the screen door, "Pastor, did you mean that I should quit my job and stay at home?"

My pastor and his wife invited me in and assured me that he had not been singling out anyone, but was going through the book of Titus and "that verse was just there." We talked and they prayed with me and advised me to continue to wait on the Lord.

As I left and headed toward downtown Montgomery to my job, I thought, "Wait on the Lord, nothing. I have to get my peace back." How impulsive I must have appeared to my boss as I marched into his office and tearfully declared, "I have to quit work."

"Don't you like your job here?"

"I love it."

"Have I offended you in some way?"

"Oh, no, I enjoy working for you."

"Isn't the money satisfactory?"

"My goodness yes. I especially love the money. But God told me to quit." Then I explained that I had recently become a Christian and what God had been showing me during the night. I added that God hadn't actually spoken out loud, but I knew I was hearing that I was to be a keeper at home.

Mr. D.'s face broke into a big smile and he said, "Well, young lady, I'm not a man to argue with God. I too am a Christian."

That was just how difficult *and* how easy it was that day. I agreed to stay long enough for them to hire a replacement and to train her. I had no earthly idea how Marvin and I would manage financially, but I was about to have my first lesson in trusting God for something other than my home in heaven.

Some years ago I wrote a story for Redbook magazine espousing my views on women. I argued that women are just as intelligent and hard-working as men, so why should they stay home?

I believed that good parents provided a safe home, clothes, food, and enough money to give children the best. I believed it was in the best interest of my children to make as much money as possible to secure the finest education and environment for meeting the right kind of friends. I believed that some women were cut out to be homebodies but that if you had an especially good mind and the ability to handle an outside job you wouldn't harm your children by hiring caretakers. I certainly didn't understand what nurturing was all about. I didn't realize that it was the day-by-day, moment-by-moment contact that gave a child security.

A home to me was a place where you all met at the end of the day to regroup and recoup, and I had some idea that a good home life and well-adjusted children would just evolve naturally. I must have been a little too callous as I described a few friends of mine who dragged through their day in grimy housecoats, nursing black coffee and watching soap operas while their ironing reached Grand Teton heights.

It was not until years later that I realized that these women who appeared lazy and nonproductive to me had been better mothers by their sheer availability. They weren't so organized and scheduled that they couldn't listen to their children. They were there to kiss bruised knees and to solve the neighborhood fights I left to strangers. Many of these women have raised their children and have gone on to receive master's degrees in teaching; some earned nursing degrees, and one is a manufacturer's representative for a chemical company, a position heretofore exclusively occupied by males. These women can enjoy their new freedom and sense of accomplishment to the fullest, knowing that their children are able to function in the world to their fullest potential.

My article was returned with a brief note: "Too caustic; the American woman won't buy that!"

The purpose of this book is to share a bit of my walk down a new path after that major decision to become a keeper at home—a decision that has led me into a deeper study of the Word of God. I have also been privileged to speak to women's groups and individual women on this subject. The conclusion that I have come to is that God would have me encourage young Christian mothers to choose to be keepers of the home, to take care of their children and to trust God to take care of their financial and other needs.

I don't pretend to have all the answers and I hadn't intended to write a book. But at a retreat I was counseling women between sessions and, as I listened to them tell of their personal and family problems, I felt an overwhelming sense of the need to share my own experience. Many of their problems were clearly caused by working outside the home. I was so saddened and burdened for them that I decided not to give my final talk—one that I love to give, which makes the audience laugh and aims to draw the listener to love and walk more closely with the Lord. I sensed that God wanted me to address the subject of working women, but I didn't know quite how I was to do this. I had not formulated a message, and I had no clear thoughts on what to say. I prayed and asked the Lord to take over and lead me to say what *He* wanted me to say. I was so nervous that I don't remember what I did say, but I was reassured the following spring when the same church group asked me to be their guest speaker for their annual mother-daughter banquet. Following that delightful occasion, the minister's wife asked, "Did you hear what happened after your talk at the retreat?" I responded by saying that I hadn't heard. She then related the astounding fact that nearly every working woman in that group had quit her job to be a keeper at home. I was deeply moved to hear this.

Then the women told me thrilling stories of how they were trusting God to meet their needs and how He was doing it. They shared how they were really getting to know their children and running their homes like they were the most important places on earth. Many were in tears and thanked me over and over again.

I was glad that story turned out well, but I had no intention of trying to repeat it. My luck would run out for sure, and I knew at least half of my audiences would be working women. Basically, I want everyone to love me. I am too insecure to get involved in a battle. But the Lord seemed to be telling me to give the message at other places.

In Memphis at a large women's conference, I again spoke on the subject, along with Phyllis Schlafly and Beverly LaHaye. Bev encouraged me to share as honestly and as compassionately as possible. I was aware that some in the audience would be bothered that I was out speaking but telling other women to stay home and keep their families. I assured them that the only difference between us at that point was that I was standing and they were sitting, and that I only speak an average of twice a month out of town. The rest of the time I am home scrubbing toilets, wiping up spills, but more importantly, nurturing a family, doing laundry, etc.

This is what I am hearing these days: "Thanks for saying it like it is. I have been trying to decide whether to quit my job or not. For my children's sake I'm going to do it."

"I'm a young wife with no children, but I want to stay home and be a housewife. Up till today I have felt guilty not working. Thank you."

"I feel that I, as well as many others, just needed that push in the right direction. We don't know who to listen to anymore."

"Please pray for me because I want to stay home with my children, but my husband wants me to work."

As I listen to what women are saying, I now know that thousands of women are working not because they want to, but because they feel pressure to do so. I also am aware that inflation has really hurt the average family. What about others? Does God plan for some women to have careers in the fields of medicine, law and science that would be impossible to pursue if twenty years were subtracted for family responsibilities?

The reason for working are many, and just as God dealt personally with me, He must deal personally with you. My purpose is not to say, "This is the only way, walk ye in it." Rather, I hope by sharing some of my search to know God's will for my life and understand His purpose for me and my family, that you may find help and support for your own search.

Caroline Bird lists eight types of women in her book *The Two-Pay-Check Marriage*:

Traditional homemakers agree with their husbands that a wife should stay home. *Defiant homemakers* insist on staying at home, even though their husbands want them to work. *Submissive home-*

makers want to work, but their husbands want them to stay at home. *Reluctant homemakers* want to work and their husbands agree, but a family problem or lack of training holds them back. *Reluctant working wives* wish they didn't have to work, but their financial situation demands it. *Submissive working wives* want to keep house, but their husbands want them to work. *Defiant working wives* work because they want to, although their husbands don't like it. *Contemporary working wives* are working, and that's what both they and their husbands want. [1]

Whether or not you find yourself in that list, I hope you *will* classify yourself as the type most ignored by all surveys: *The searching Christian wife* who is seeking to understand and obey God's will for her and her family.

Perhaps in your desire to be the perfect wife and mother you find yourself stretched to the limit. Perhaps, like me, you need to give up trying to be Superwoman, who, despite a demanding career, insists on controlling everything at home, participating in community affairs, producing perfect children, and entertaining lavishly. That will surely take a toll on your marriage, your children, and your health. But what should go? Children?

Are we, as Caroline Bird predicts, headed toward a smaller world?

> The most probable future—and the happiest, too will be a small world. There are many reasons to believe that the birth rate will continue to drop until the population of the United States begins shrinking some time during the next century. [2]

Should the traditional family be buried?

> "Ad hoc" families? Yale sociologist Rosabeth Kanter saw the emergence of what she called a "post-biological" family held together by a "quality of feeling rather than a biological tie." If feeling is the tie, then a family can be assembled for a specific purpose, the way unacquainted musicians can get together to play string quartets. [3]

Can this statement be true?

Most of us are learning that roles can be changed like clothing, and that temporary relationships are less likely to be exploitative and uncaring than those that have biological or economic consequences.[4]

How unlike Edith Schaeffer's description of the family that is. In her fine book, *What Is a Family?*, Mrs. Schaeffer pictures the family as a mobile—"the most versatile, ever-changing mobiles that exists" . . . "an artwork that takes years, even generations, to produce, but which is never finished."

A family is a grouping of individuals who are *affecting* each other intellectually, emotionally, spiritually, physically, psychologically. No two years, no two months or no two days is there the exact same blend or mix within the family, as each individual person is changing.[5]

Mrs. Schaeffer says the family is an "art form", an "exciting art career, because an art form needs work."

Well, then should femininity go? Are we to believe that we are being held down or back by our "accident of sex"? Ms. Bird states that men have always known that sex needn't be forever, but it wasn't until the 1970s that women learned it too.

. . . Sexual experimentation was no longer initiated by men alone. Successful, financially independent women were sometimes shocked by their own sexiness and the ease with which they accepted variant sex practices and partners who would have been inappropriate husbands.[6]

She foresees a more unisex, male society as women become more like men in their sexual experience, choice of clothing, and the development of character traits such as rationality, competition, and concern for achievement. "Femininity, it appears, is not an inborn female sex characteristic, but an artifact of powerlessness that will never be missed."

Ms. Bird says that in a revolt against double standards, it must be determined which standard—male or female—will prevail. In her opinion, it will be the male pattern that will apply to both sexes: "Early initiation into full sexual activity, a variety of partners, experimentation with differing practices and active solicitation of male partners will be expected of women."

You may be asking, as I did, "What about the children?"

> Better selection of parents should greatly reduce the problems psychia-
> trists attribute to feelings of being unloved or unwanted, to say nothing
> of the damage done by mothers ordered to dish out tender, loving care
> when they don't feel like it. [7]

Ms. Bird says professionals will "sell Congress on funding direct
services to children, which like the public school system, will be
available to all, regardless of need." She foresees all children getting their teeth straightened, going to summer camp and receiving
medical care at the public expense.

Are women really willing to give up the dream of a home, a long
marriage, and a family, all for a paycheck? I hardly think so. But I
also think that many Christian women haven't stopped to count
the cost of working outside the home as efficiently as the women
surveyed by Ms. Bird did.

Yes, the conscientious woman is confronted with a dilemma as
she weighs alternatives. Many factors contribute to helping her
make a choice: should she work or should she concentrate all her
energies on being a fulltime keeper of the home?

The thing that disturbs me when I read books like *The Two-
Paycheck Marriage* is that I believe many of Ms. Bird's predictions
can come true. The *Brave New World* of Huxley's that we snickered
at is upon us. The factor so important and so vitally needed to
preserve and support the traditional marriage, family, and home in
this not-so-brave world is the *female factor*.

The thing that thrills me is that woman—once she has achieved
the exciting knowledge of, as Elisabeth Elliot says, "Not who am I?
but Whose am I?"—is destined to forge ahead following a divine
blueprint to discover the wonders of our daily new world.

In succeeding chapters we will explore not only what society says
about the woman, the marriage, the home, the family and working,
but what the Bible has to say about it and hopefully what your heart
will say about it.

Since writing that article I submitted to *Redbook* years ago, I have done a total about-face. Not that my views regarding women's intelligence and abilities have changed, but I have had second thoughts about women leaving their homes to work unless it is absolutely necessary.

You see, a mobile taken apart, not moving with the natural sway of life is no longer an art form; it is only bits and pieces placed somewhere else. The question the female factor in each household must answer is, how are the bits and pieces of her family to be strung together?

2. Whatever Happened to Titus 2?

> Only take heed to thyself, and keep thy soul diligently,
> lest thou forget the things which thine eyes have seen
> and lest they depart from thy heart . . . but teach
> them . . .
>
> Deuteronomy 4:9

Since the early 1970s, while the whirlwind feminist movement, misappropriately called "Women's Lib," has dominated magazines, newspapers, and TV talk shows, a strange conflict has been going on inside my head. I too have become incensed when seeing women browbeaten, not provided for, abused and ordered around by men who were selfish, and insensitive. I have seen discrimination in employment first hand. At times I have wanted to shake my fist in the face of men who were subjecting women to sexual harassment. Yet regarding defense of the family, I am convinced that the woman, the wife and mother—the female factor—must maintain her position, in armed combat, if necessary.

I would be quick to say a loud amen to equality that will make life better for a woman. I do believe that women deserve equal pay for equal work, and that *is* the law in our country covered by the Civil Rights Act of 1964, the Equal Pay Act of 1963, and the Equal Opportunity Act of 1972. I agree with the feminists that women have in many cases been treated as hated stepchildren when it comes to getting the jobs they are qualified for and deserve. But that kind of discrimination is dealt with in the Comprehensive

Health and Manpower Training Act of 1971, the Comprehensive Employment and Training Act of 1973 and the Federal Equal Credit Opportunity Act of 1975.

Passage of the Equal Rights Amendment could not erase social injustice to women in all areas of life. But examining the issues it has brought into the spotlight *has* exposed unfair, unjust practices. Positive, good, and long overdue improvements for women can be credited to the feminist movement—fairer hiring practices, better working conditions, and awareness of sexual harassment on the job.

But something still makes me uneasy. Are the women's liberationists going too far? Have they become intoxicated with power, too pushy, and too vocal as they seek to speak for the whole of womanhood? Are they, in fact, becoming as obnoxious as the selfish, insensitive man who barks orders at his browbeaten wife?

Dale Evans says:

> I used to laugh at the thing called "Women's Lib," but I'm not laughing now. In its first days, it seemed logical enough to me that women should stand in equality with men; back then it appeared to be another phase of the fight for women's liberation started on the political front, by such women as Emmeline Parkhurst, Carrie Chapman Catt, and Susan B. Anthony; but the modern lib movement has grown into something quite different from that. Today a really radical element is driving the lib horses. I hear them shouting for some causes that are insignificant to me. . . .
>
> When I ponder the platforms of some of these radical feminists—the easy abortions; the demand of the right to "do their thing" no matter who gets hurt as they do it, the "liberated" women spouting about their "free lifestyle", I get a little sick and I ask myself,—Dear God—what happens to the children of such free spirits?[1]

That's where my conflict comes in too—the children. I espoused the "lib" philosophy twenty years ago, long before it was fashionable. I was out there pushing for the best job, equal pay, and all the self-improvement methods I could indulge in. No crime in that. *But what about the children, the home, the church, and society as a whole?*

I had already written the first draft of this book when a friend gave me Edith Schaeffer's book *What is a Family.* What she had to say helped me understand my uneasiness.

> I think we can see the whole race as one in which true truth is to be handed over like the flag in a relay race, from generation to generation. . . . We are responsible for "handing on the flag" and for being very careful not to drop it—or to drop out—because of our responsibility to the next generation.[2]

In Titus 2 Paul exhorts his helper to teach his church "sound doctrine" so that they in turn can teach. Before the Word of God was available to every person, it had to be handed down by example, word of mouth, and teaching. I believe God has definitely called some of us to be full-time homemakers so that we will by example hand the Christian flag over to the next generation in order that the race not be stopped.

Until now, I had no idea that I was involved in a humanistic cultural revolution. I thought I would be the exception to the rule. But in 1980, 46.6 percent of all American mothers with children under six were either employed or looking for work, the Women's Bureau of the U.S. Labor Department reported. This meant that some 7.5 million preschool children were in need of daycare, according to *Family Weekly,* April 5, 1981.

Five years ago I was taking a college course with a cute, red-headed woman five years younger than myself. We became friendly sparring partners in the feminist arena, much to the delight of our liberal professor who got my number when she spotted me wearing double-knits instead of jeans. I don't know if she was keeping score on who was the most fulfilled, but I did get an insight into a type of modern woman I had not seen before. My friend had been divorced for several years and had custody of three children ranging in age from seven to fifteen. I wasn't prepared for the shock of hearing that she hitchhiked to school everyday in skin tight jeans and halter tops. When I showed an earnest concern for her safety during a time when the rape and murder of young women in Tampa was a frequent occurrence, she laughed and told me that was how she met her various sleeping partners. "I couldn't stand to think that I could

only be loved by one man," she said. I looked her squarely in the
eye, feeling an overwhelming sense of contentment. "Well, honey,
it is obvious that you have never been loved by the right man."

Believe it or not, we two birds of a different hue had some warm,
honest times of sharing, and I found that under her rough exterior
beat a mother's heart concerned that her fifteen-year-old daughter
was already sleeping around and into drugs.

The main source of this woman's discontent was obvious. Instead
of her strong belief in reincarnation and transcendental meditation,
with a little Bible thrown in for good measure, she needed a Savior.
When I asked her who in the world she fellowshiped or worshiped
with, she said that no one believed like she did, and thus she was
very lonely. I am sorry that I was not able to win her to Christ, but I
am more sorry for her children, who have aged five years since
then. The freedom purchased by their mother may be bankrupting
them psychologically.

Even before I became a Christian and while I was indulging in
my "free-thinking" binges and searching for the ever-elusive self-
fulfillment, I too was concerned about my children. But while I
loved them, they were definitely a hindrance to my career. Then
when I first became a Christian, I trusted Christ as my Savior *and* to
make me a better mother, but I didn't consider the matter of my
working to be an issue that concerned Him.

Soon after becoming a Christian I began studying the Bible in
earnest in classes and meetings in our church. Under the good
teaching of our pastor we became well schooled in doctrines of the
faith—God, sin, the Blood of Christ, the Resurrection—and realized that they were basic and essential to the Christian faith.

When we began to learn about the Christian walk it was a
different story for me. More times than I care to recall I became
uncomfortable—yes, even convicted—about areas in my life that
were off-base. While holding down a job made it harder to live the
Christian life, I continued to work. Then came one memorable
Sunday when I was caught off guard and Titus 2 forcefully impacted
my life. I could not get away from the implications of the part that
says women are "To be discreet, chaste, keepers at home, good,
obedient to their own husbands . . ." (v. 5).

For years I have been buying and handing out books on how to improve your marriage, but I have found precious few clear-cut admonitions in such books to young women, urging them to put careers on the back burner while their children are still being molded. When Titus 2 is mentioned at all, the "keeper at home" portion is generally interpreted to mean that a woman should be a good housekeeper. Recently I heard a respected, well-known Bible teacher speak on Titus, and when he arrived at the "keeper at home" phrase he whizzed over it, mumbling something about keeping a clean house. When I saw him later, I reflected my unbelief, "You had five thousand people in there; why didn't you tell it like it is?"

"Couldn't you feel the audience go stiff on me when I had the working wives hold up their hands?" he said.

Now while I believe that keeping a house clean is important, a deeper look into that passage reveals the importance of the female factor in the home.

As I began to take a deeper look, I started asking myself some questions. I noticed that the chapter begins: "But speak thou the things which become *sound doctrine,*" or "which are suitable to sound doctrine." Clearly, Titus 2 is a book of instructions concerning Christian behavior, domestic relations, and lifestyles of both older and younger men and women of faith. God, through Paul, is saying that older women in the faith are to teach the younger women some things basic to life, and especially living the Christian life.

Many career choices are available to women today. But if we, as women, choose marriage *and* a career, then those of us who have learned the truth of Titus 2, are to warn younger women that they risk much in the process. One woman has described it as "bartering golden hours." What do we receive in exchange for leaving our babies and toddlers in the hands of a sitter for eight or nine hours a day? Certainly a paycheck (and that will be greatly diminished by the time we pay the sitter)—but what else? We have lost out on precious moments with those little ones who are little actually for such a short time (in comparison to the rest of their lives). *Pass the relay flag.*

Dr. James Dobson, when asked if all women should marry, have children and stay home, replied,

> A woman should feel free to choose the direction her life will take. In no sense should she be urged to raise a family and abandon her own career or educational objectives, if this is not her desire. . . . My strong criticism, then, is not with those who choose a nonfamily life style for themselves. Rather it is aimed at those who abandon their parental responsibility after the choice has been made.[3]

Why are Christian women, of all people, being duped into jumping into quicksand all the while those who don't even claim to be Christian are warning us not to:

> "Working outside the home is killing me by inches, I feel like a bug stuck on a pin."
>
> "As I grew up, I dreamed of having a home of my own to fix up, to cherish, to fill with my handmade things. I dreamed of preparing good meals and putting out a white, sweet-smelling wash. I dreamed of a husband to love and care for and children to rear."
>
> "What I have is a dingy mobile home I am too tired to clean. A husband who sits home watching TV and eating and whose sole contribution to my life is driving me to and from work."
>
> "This happened so slowly that I was trapped before I sensed the danger. When we married, we had nothing. He said it was hard to get going and he would appreciate help for a bit, so I went to work. We were to have a home faster that way. Then he needed a newer car and a boat, and inflation came, and I'm stuck."
>
> A high-powered professional woman who looks as if she had the world by the tail can feel like a bug stuck on a pin, too. "Private law practice is insecure, so two incomes are necessary," an attorney wrote. . . ."Many men find it 'challenging.' The men can *have* it."
>
> "I wish there were a way out. Unfortunately, hubby is liberated and says I must support myself. . . ."[4]

I am not for one moment suggesting that women involved in a career or even in the women's movement love their husbands, children, or homes any less than those of us who opt for staying home. I am suggesting that when I left my children with a sitter from 7:30 A.M. until 5:00 P.M., I didn't have much left to give to my children when I picked them up. It did help that for several years my children were cared for by an aunt who had children the same age and who really loved them. Later I had a sitter who came to my home and kept them. So my children didn't suffer from being stuck in an overpopulated day-care center, but they did suffer from having a mother who just wanted to get them fed and tucked in bed.

Most of the years I worked outside the home it was clearly a case of my doing what I wanted, rather than doing what was best for my family. Even though I particularly enjoyed my job as executive secretary to a group of psychologists, I can't say that I received any long-lasting feelings of fulfillment from it. I wondered about the more successful career women who were obviously making it on their own. Then I began to read of women who seemed to have it all, like Taylor Caldwell, one of the most successful writers in the world. When asked by *Family Weekly* whether she felt solid satisfaction in knowing that her novel *Captains and Kings* was to be seen as a nine-hour television production, she replied:

> There is no solid satisfaction in any career for a woman like myself. There is no home, no true freedom, no hope, no joy, no expectation for tomorrow, no contentment. I would rather cook a meal for a man and bring him his slippers and feel myself in the protection of his arms than have all the citations and awards and honors I have received worldwide, including the ribbon of the Legion of Honor and my property and my bank accounts. [5]

Former Israeli Premier Golda Meir, perhaps the highest achiever and most notable career woman of our time, said that "having a baby is the most fulfilling thing a woman can ever do." [6]

I know what I am saying will make some women angry even as these things angered me when I first heard them. Part of me still wants to say, "Do whatever makes you happy." I *know* just getting out of the house sometimes seems like the most important thing in the world.

We all have days at home that make laying sewer pipe look

interesting by comparison. In fact, I'm having just such a day myself, trying to juggle the time to give medicine to three flu-ridden
family members, waiting for a counselee who is threatening suicide,
needing to go to school and pick up Matt's homework sometime
before I take mother-in-law to the doctor, and prepare dinner for
the whole shebang. The Monday laundry is piled as high as Mount
Everest and dust is rolling around like a tumbleweed. I was almost
sorry the sun finally came out because in the dark it all looked
better. Sure, I want to scream PHOOEY at a day like today. But then
I ask myself, Would it be any easier if I had a job? Of course not! I
would just have one more thing to do. I'd have to arrange for days
off or find someone to take the kids to the doctor or go to the
drugstore. I'd have to get a sitter to stay home with Matt, and on
and on.

If what Caroline Bird says is true—that by 1990, two-thirds of all
women are expected to be working—the one-third staying home
will be in a fix trying to fill the blank spaces left by the others!

Often, after I've spoken at a retreat, young mothers with several
children will come up to talk to me. I look into their seeking faces
and wish I had a magical solution to make things easier for them.
Especially do the young Christian mothers hope for some spiritual
advice that will whisk them through the demanding years of day-
after-day feeding, diapering, stopping fights, healing hurts, answering a multitude of questions, and yearning for a few moments of
privacy. I usually just squeeze their hands, smile, and remind them
they do have the advantage of a life controlled by the Holy Spirit.
And, I add, "I know what you are going through; I had four little
ones too. I know you get tired and confused, but I really admire
what you are doing. It is the single, most important task God gives
a woman. But, much of what you are living must just be gotten
through. Millions of others have gotten through it and you will too.
You may be really surprised in a few years to see that you have really
been a great mother."

Those of us who are qualified by virtue of (1) our physical age,
and (2) our lives lived as "older" Christians, don't want to be
"preachy" or to set ourselves up as perfect examples. We're not
trying to make working women feel guilty, for we recognize that

many young women must work in these days of a tight economy. And certainly this is not intended as a put-down of the many who are able to handle a career and family too. But if ever Christian families were needed on the face of this earth, it is now. We are needed to multiply and replenish the earth with strong, well-adjusted, responsible individuals who will be our progeny. And that is the challenge facing us today.

In the Garden of Eden God didn't tell Eve she couldn't eat fruit; she could have it all—all but one. Satan convinced her that the reason God didn't want her to eat that one was because it was the best. She obeyed his urging to "do her own thing." It wasn't the end of Eve, only the end of God's *perfect* plan for her life, and she took us all down with her.

The feminists are not wrong about women being just as intelligent, capable, and creative as men, but I believe they are cheating many women out of God's *perfect* plan for their lives by urging them to grab the wrong apple first.

The female factor is too important to God's whole economy not to consider her choices carefully.

3. Human Zoos Need Keepers Too!

"She riseth also . . . and giveth meat to her household. . . ."

Proverbs 31:15

During those anxious, unknowing years before I hung up my Superwoman jersey, I often wished I could lock my children in their rooms and throw in Twinkies every couple of hours. There were nights when I felt like the bloody remains of a lion attack. I did everything but hold up a chair and crack a bullwhip to keep the hissing kittens from eating each other alive. I definitely had a human zoo to contend with.

When it got to be too much for me during my staying-home periods, I would explain to my husband that I was clearly slipping out of reality and I needed outside diversion. I would choose as carefully as I could someone to contend with cage-cleaning and bowl-filling, and I would jump in my car and get on a highway already jammed with coffee-primed working mothers.

Some of the job titles I have had would give me a temporarily inflated image of myself and I would congratulate myself for being able to swing a career all the while the cute, cuddly "animals" at home were swinging from the chandeliers, out of my view. I was secretary to the director of research at a human research lab, secretary to the assistant to the president at a State Farm Bureau, secretary to the ordinance officer at an Army base, office manager for two dentists in an exclusive practice.

To feel that God had asked me to give up those titles was bad enough, but to be labeled a "keeper" really took a swipe at my self-image.

Somehow, during my struggle with finding God's will for my life at that time, I erroneously concluded that if I obeyed God's calling and became a keeper at home, things would be different. Perhaps my home wouldn't resemble a zoo after all, and all sorts of images came to mind of a dream castle in perfect order. I didn't believe enough in the images to spout them, however, because after making the decision to stay at home, whenever anyone asked me what I did, I would turn red in the face, lower my head, and mutter, "I'm just a housewife." I felt almost apologetic that I wasn't contributing something meaningful and worthwhile to society.

And there *were* days when I felt like moving out and not leaving a stocked refrigerator or a forwarding address—days when the toilet was overflowing with the toys, three children were down with mumps, a cat was giving birth, and Marvin was bringing company home for dinner.

Some days I stared up into heaven and cried out to God, "Why me, Lord? What did I do to deserve this? Anybody with half a brain and a strong stomach and back can do this; I was made for something better." When two-year-old Matt put three pounds of hamburger into the dryer full of white clothes, I felt as if I were at the end of the line. As I picked off the tiny little meatballs from my husband's best white shirt and rinsed out the blood spots, I remembered another time when I had to remove dried play-dough from my best silk dress. I wanted to stop cleaning up fingerpaint on the walls and write a big blue message on the front of our house, "HELP, I'M BEING HELD CAPTIVE!"

Those were the years when I was obeying God and being a keeper. The animals still hissed and squealed and barked, so what difference did it make who kept them?

I think I found the answer not long ago. Just for curiosity's sake I looked up the word *keeper* in *Webster's New World Dictionary*. The more I read, the farther back my shoulders went and the higher my head raised. I believe if you will read these definitions with one finger underlining Titus 2:5 and one eye focused on your home and family, you too will have a chest swelling with a new pride:

> To go on *maintaining,* to *protect, guard, defend, watch over, take care;* to *maintain in good order or condition, preserve,* to *provide for; support;* to *carry on; conduct, manage;* to *continue to have or hold, not lose or give up;* to *stay in or at* (a path, course or place) to *stay in a specific position,* to *continue, go on, persevere, hold oneself back, refrain,* to *stay fresh, not spoil, last, care, charge, custody, food, shelter, support.* [1]

I began to see right there in the dictionary why following God's prescribed plan is so important. There are unsolved problems in so many homes because we forget the importance of the female factor. I believe the female is superior to the male in carrying out the mission of keeping the home and family. I don't believe a man can hold a candle to a woman when it comes to organization, defense, maintenance, stability, perseverance, self-control, and unselfishness in connection with the home. God has endued woman with the physical strength and mental acumen to carry out a job that in the business world would require at least ten experts. To that He has added a double portion of emotional sensitivity to deal with the variety of emotional beings under her roof.

I have heard various people try to put a price tag on what a homemaker-mother is worth. The lowest lately was $16,000, and the highest was between $50,000 and $80,000 per year. I frankly don't believe it is possible to accurately evaluate in dollars and cents what a real homemaker is worth. But, at the very time when men are realizing a woman's importance as a homemaker, multitudes of women are hanging up their aprons and going elsewhere to earn a dose of self-importance as well as a salary.

If I were to make the definition of keeper into a personal declaration it would sound like: "I am to maintain my home and protect and defend it from all its enemies. I am to stay in my position that no other take it over. I must continue to keep it fresh and not let anything spoil it. I will hold myself back from endeavors that cause

me to give up the best part." I believe if we could see the preciousness of the home from God's point of view homemakers would be
elevated to new heights of value and importance.

Whether or not families will exist fifty years from now seems to
lie in our hands. God seems to have given *us* the responsibility for
perpetuating a lifestyle that is to be cherished.

If we could ask the opinion of working women in Russia or
China—whom we usually see pictured all dressed in the same dingy
gray or blue—they would probably tell us how happy they would be
to have a home of their own where they could run their corner of
the world. They must wish they didn't have to give up their children to government day-care centers practically from the time they
are born. They would probably exchange places with us in an
instant.

If we don't jealously guard our right to a home, run autonomously
and according to our desires, who will guard it? If we don't opt for
the privilege of having our children home with us at least until age
five, and if we don't care who watches the children, who will?

I believe the militant feminist groups who have been so vocal in
their efforts have not clearly understood where their march could
lead women of the future. I believe the changes they have been
advocating deprive us of our right to be what God intended us to
be. No doubt when they read this portion about being a "keeper,"
they will not dig into all that that means, but liken it to slave work
or the caretaking of a zoo, much as I earlier thought. Their purpose
has been, I am sure, to equalize women with men and to elevate
women to more important places. But instead they are in fact
secretly robbing us.

1. In trying to neuterize our country by eliminating traditional
role models, they have successfully removed from many school
textbooks any reference to a woman as a homemaker. She may be
shown as a salesperson or a lineperson; but if there is work to be
shown in the home, it is usually beside a man with an apron on,
"sharing equally in the work." On the other hand, women are
depicted as actively engaged "in exciting worthwhile pursuits."
Clearly the implication is that being a "keeper at home" is not
worthwhile. Women who are confused as to their own feelings and

who want to be "with it" are buying the whole bag without considering what they might be throwing away.

2. Their work for passage of the Equal Rights Amendment would
have nullified the laws requiring a husband to support his wife and
children. The Bible clearly teaches in 1 Timothy 5:8 that a man
who does not provide for his own house is worse than an un-
believer. This has not happened, however, and in the laws of our
country the woman is provided for so that she may legally have the
right to stay home and raise her own babies and children.

> One of the most fundamental duties imposed by the law of domestic
> relations is that which requires a man to support his wife and family. In
> some jurisdictions, the duty to support is imposed on the husband by
> statute. . . . But it exists apart from statute, as a duty arising out of
> marital relationship. . . .
> The duty of the husband to support his wife arises out of the marital
> relationship and continues during the existence of that relationship.
> The duty of support is consistent with the husband's financial ability,
> and in accordance with the station in life to which he has accustomed
> his family. . . .
> The duty of a husband to support his wife and family, arising out of
> the marriage relationship, exists without reference to the wife's separate
> estate or independent means, and the husband has no right to resort to
> her separate estate or means, as a general rule, to support her or the
> family. A husband's duty to support his wife also exists without refer-
> ence to what she can earn by her own labor, and he has no right to
> demand that she earn all that she can in order to contribute to her
> support.[2]

Now, most of us do not enter the marital relationship with a long
list of "his" and "her" duties tied around our necks. Yet we may
rather blindly, through love, decide to give our all and wear ourselves out, providing what we can to build our relationship. Some
time after our honeymoon, however, our eyes open and we find
that we each have inherited some duties that seem hard or unfair.
For this reason it became necessary to delegate legally some of the
larger duties that affect the well-being of the whole family.

Colorado has adopted a State Equal Rights Amendment as part of their state constitution. This amendment gives a preview of what "absolute equality" means in terms of marriage. They amended the existing law requiring the husband to support his wife and children, changing the terms *woman, wife, husband, man* (considered "sexist") into *person* or *spouse*. So now under Colorado law the wife bears equal weight in the obligation to support her family, under threat of criminal conviction of a class-five felony.

Equality regardless of sex doesn't just mean equal pay for equal work (which, by the way, is *already* the law). It also means husband and wife share equal responsibility for caring for the children, and in effect will remove criminal liability from the man who neglects and abandons his family. Women following the feminist Pied Piper may get more than they bargained for. In the opinion of many male legal minds in our country, it will eventually benefit men no longer to have the responsibility of providing for a family. Not all men would be so irresponsible and selfish as to hop from bed to bed with no commitments, of course. But I know firsthand of cases in which the husband has never held his wife in an elevated place and discounts her job at home as worthless and I know of many who have never supported their family. Countless women are angry because in return for their love and dedication they have received abuse either in the form of physical beatings or mental cruelty. I am sympathetic, but I am simply asking them not to take their anger out on the rest of us by advocating legislation with such destructive potential.

3. By demanding that the managing and care of the home must be equally shared by husband and wife, the feminists are really asking the wife to surrender her power. *American Jurisprudence, 2d* states:

> The husband's obligation of support requires him to provide his wife with a place of abode that will be deemed a suitable home when considered in the light of modern standards . . . and the means and earning power of the husband . . . the control of which she need not relinquish or share with others, but a home in which she is the mistress.[3]

"Mistress" in the context of this law does not mean a woman
who has sexual relations with, and may be supported by, a man to
whom she is not married. Rather, it means a woman who rules
others or controls something, specifically a woman head of a household, or something regarded as feminine that has power or control.

Isn't it interesting that women have been given by law a domain
over which to rule, as a queen bee, if you will? Even with our
understanding of male authority, Christian wives are given this
control by Scripture. And yet, women are by droves, abdicating
their power, abandoning their hives, to become mere "worker
bees" in another's hive.

Early in my marriage I made an assumption that, like my mother,
I had certain areas of right and responsibility, such as care of the
clothing, decorating the home, and preparing the meals. Now, I
didn't go to the local department store and purchase a golden
scepter to rule with. I may look like royal rulership in some of the
housecoats I wear when Marvin is out of town, but I assure you my
influence and power is exerted in quiet ways and not by barking
orders. I believe the Bible clearly teaches that my husband's place is
directly under God as leader of our family. I am placed directly
under my husband's authority, but with that placement comes considerable power. I don't have to snatch and grab the power; it
belongs to me. I am the queen bee in my home, and there are
certain areas in my hive that you'd better not mess with unless you
want to get stung. These are important to me.

I am sure someone is asking the question: "What if the woman
has strong leadership abilities and the husband doesn't, and he
wants her to lead?" Does he really? I don't pretend to know all the
answers and while I am drawing mainly on personal experience, I
have seen marriages that seemed to be that way. On closer examination, however, the man, while perhaps timid, *did* want to be the
leader. A marriage like this needs special grace from the Lord as the
leader-wife voluntarily yields that leadership to a person who may
not be as adept. For the sake of her husband's manhood and her
respect for him in the future, I believe the transition will produce
good results. Because a man doesn't desire conflict, he may go on

and on letting the wife lead while not necessarily being satisfied or happy about it.

While in nearly every area of life my husband has stronger leader-ship ability, I had definite ideas of how I wanted my marriage, home, family, etc., to be. How was *he* to know unless I told him what to do to make it happen? In other words, while not actually ruling, I can be pretty bossy when it serves my purposes. On the other hand, my natural leader husband, hating conflict, spoiling me rather than fighting, would give in to whatever I wanted. Talk about role reversal!

Hearing of and trying to obey the submission principle early in my Christian life brought confusion. I would tack on a submissive spirit and piously ask Marvin's opinion on everything from what I should buy at the grocery to when I should shampoo the rug. Rather than kiss my hand for such sweetness, he would let me know in no uncertain terms that his mind was filled with debits and credits and tying up sales deals. He indicated that he was perfectly happy with my remaining queen bee of the home.

Some working women put me to shame as they manage to juggle orthodontist appointments, baseball practice, and gourmet meals without so much as a broken nail. You may be one of these, and I am certainly not trying to teach you anything. Rather, I am speak-ing to the young Christian woman who is trying to decide between a career at home or outside the home. If your working means putting food before your children, I would agree that is what you must do. But, if you are yearning for a color TV or an extra car or even just to get away from the zoo, I pray you will seek God's will.

A color TV can be purchased at any time, but the nurturing period of your children lasts just so long and you get only one chance at it. A second car may take you more places, but what your kids receive from a mom at home will take them more places in the future. Learning to keep that human zoo of yours may be just what you need in the way of training for the future. Some could run corporations, fine hotels and restaurants on the experience they have gained.

If woman, the female factor, who is so gifted for the job of keeper, refuses self-pity or cursing the fact that she was born female, she is free to see God's hand in preparing her for the future. If she remains free from anger and is open-minded and open-hearted, God will be able to reveal talents and desires that may be hidden.

Years ago, while spending hours each day on my front porch, watching the children play, I began dabbling with oil paints. I'm no Grandma Moses or Michelangelo, but I really enjoy it and when I have more time I plan to really get into it. So far, it has enabled me to give gifts from my heart to friends and family.

As a writer I'm no Shakespeare, but then he didn't have to juggle writing between hanging a load of clothes and stirring the soup. Rather than indulging in the occasional anger I feel over having been a keeper for so many years, I take whatever hours are mine and try to learn more of the craft of writing.

Over the kitchen table and a coffee mug and out of past heartaches and joys, I am learning another important skill: to be a counselor to other mothers who feel like failures.

A distress call came from a young mother of three here from Australia while her husband studied for his doctorate. Depressed at the discovery of her third pregnancy, she cried to me, "I came here to learn so I could go back and be used of God. And here I am, just wasting time and money by staying home!" When I asked her who she wanted to help in Australia, she said, "Other women." "What do most of those women do?" I asked. "Why," she replied, "they have families and take care of their homes."

When I suggested to her that she was in school as much as her husband, a light went on. She was learning by experience the truths that God would have her share with women in like circumstances about trusting God and seeing his hand in everyday experiences. The contentment that now registers on her face is not from the fact that some of the ladies in her church are helping with their basic needs and relieving her by caring for the children sometimes, but by the fact that she has rooted out bitterness and sees her position as an important training ground.

Keeping of the home and family means different things to different people but, during the child raising days, I think there are some basic areas that are universal in nature.

1. *Home Atmosphere.* I had an important lesson in this at a friend's home recently. She invited me to sit down at her oak kitchen table to talk while she peeled potatoes.

Her preschooler interrupted her for the fifth time since I had arrived. "Mom, where are the scissors?"

Ann obviously didn't feel the irritation I felt as she smiled, "Oh, honey, I forgot to put them back after cutting out my pattern. They're on the footstool."

As Debbie turned to leave, my friend called, "When you get finished, come on in here. I've made some cookies for you."

Later, Debbie sat down next to her mother and put her head on the table. Ann rubbed her back while we continued our conversation. Shortly, Debbie dozed, and Ann seemed very content. The warm, loving atmosphere of that home was apparent.

I was reminded that I would have worked harder at that time to impress a *visitor* with the right atmosphere.

I had another friend who kept the messiest house in town, rarely got a meal together on time, ironed what clothes the children needed right before the school bus came. While maintaining better control than that is important to me, it wasn't to her. Every day when the kids got home, she sat and leisurely listened to their chatter. With four children this could take hours! All this "time-killing" made me nervous, but in the long run I learned a valuable lesson from her. The art of communication takes time and when the children feel they are worth it, the atmosphere is set at "secure."

The atmosphere of the home has nothing to do with decor or style. Rather, for the family it's a lot more than that. It's a feeling of being wanted and cared for. It's the smell of something simmering in a pot or baking in an oven. It's knowing Mom has time for listening and really being interested in how school was. It's a welcome mat for friends. It's a home that's reasonably clean but not sterile and untouchable.

For me it means that I've gotten most of my personal daily goals out of the way so my children know they are the most important people I know. I have failed so often at this I am ashamed to admit it, but through the failure I have seen the need.

2. *Meals*. Mealtimes used to be wonderful occasions where all family members regrouped and humorously shared their day. There were often long, sometimes heated discussions, and opportunities for teaching children manners and the value of certain foods.

My jogging has been an eye-opener. In the morning I see mothers dragging sleepy-eyed youngsters out the door clutching a poptart. That's breakfast.

If I jog after our dinner hour I often see those same people lugging sacks of hamburgers into the house. Judging from the paper plates and beer cans strewn around garbage cans, it appears that eating is quick, effortless, messless and probably doesn't add much to family life.

I read somewhere recently that the average father spends less than two minutes a day with his child. This could be relieved some if we re-established mealtimes. But that gets back to the female factor again.

There is a security felt by the family whose meals are planned and in some stage of preparation when the crew arrives on the scene. Again, it says, "I care for you and I am making something for you."

Even when I travel I try to keep my hand on the mealtime at home. I'm almost never gone more than three days at the longest but I prepare casseroles, soups, spaghetti, and other family favorites to leave in the freezer. I leave typed directions on the refrigerator. I prepare sandwiches and snacks for school lunches. I cut up vegetables for tossed salads and make congealed salads. The morning I leave I put something in the Crockpot—chicken that noodles can be added to, chili, pot roast, etc.

If you are a working mom, I'm sure you have found many convenient ways of preparing meals on budgeted time. I learned long ago that tonight is when I need to think about what I will serve tomorrow night. Nothing makes me more frantic than to arrive home after a day of meetings and have nothing thawed for dinner. You can have eggs only so often!

3. *Clothing*. Someone has to be in charge of purchasing and caring for the clothing a family wears. It is easier for me than for Marvin to plan that area of responsibility and carry it out. When the kids were small, I tried to buy a year ahead during the end-of-

season sales, thus saving at least half of what those same clothes would cost at regular price. Because it was my job, I could keep up with which children needed something and try to juggle it so that all four didn't need shoes in one week.

Nothing unnerves me quite like someone yelling downstairs at 7:30 A.M., "I need a clean pair of jeans in ten minutes!" The way I avoid an ulcer is by throwing a load in the washer every day. Other families delegate that responsibility, and it works well.

When I worked, Marvin did share the housework and I do believe that is fair. Many nights we would watch TV and fold diapers (diapers which, by the way, he also changed regularly).

4. *Cleaning.* Again, while I believe the female factor, the home keeper, needs to be in control of the situation, I think each member of the family needs to share in cleaning. This teaches children responsibility for their own things and instills concern for other people's property. Once they have to clean up someone else's mess you can hear them nagging the guilty party not to mess it up again.

5. *Shopping.* While I know many men who do the shopping and women who hate it, I do think it should be the woman's prerogative. Certainly it's not fair for a man to shop and then gripe because the wife doesn't prepare better meals. But each couple must have its own agreeable, *workable* situation.

There may be areas of equal importance to others, but I know that if the above five areas are neglected too long in our home it causes a strain. Do I always like it? Is it always fair? Do I always have things running smoothly? The answer to all of the above is no. But rather than having a big, loud "KEEPER AT HOME" assaulting my brain with guilt feelings, I have a comforting pat on my heart that reassures me that I am a keeper at home. Not perfect, but keeping on keeping.

Working women *can* be good keepers, but it takes emphasis on your number one priority, your family. You have to plan more, think more clearly, and work harder, but it can be done, and my hat's off to all you who are managing so well.

Perhaps you are one of many who feel pulled, like you aren't competent anywhere. I'd like to urge you to consider making a career of keeping at home. Look at your family. You may decide the

most worthwhile and meaningful contribution you can make to
society is to send into it productive, responsible young people who
will be a solution rather than a contributor to its ills.

It's a sad fact that there are some keepers at home who actually
aren't keepers at all. They schedule their day around *All My Children* and *Ryan's Hope,* and they give little hope to their own children. There are also good, Christian mothers who are so busy
"serving the Lord" that serving their family takes a back seat. It
takes more to be a "keeper" by our definition than just physically
not working outside the home. You can volunteer yourself to death.
Why do women busy themselves giving untiringly to others? Because they need to feel they are of some value. They need to know
they are making a contribution. How did homemaking slip so low
on the charts of worthwhile contributions? I don't know for sure,
but I expect the media have had a lot to do with it. But I believe
those of us who see the importance can elevate it back to its proper
place.

Still, even a mother addicted to soap operas is at home to hand
out Band-aids and put out fires.

I feel a certain frustration over young women who tell me, "Oh,
we want to learn to be good homemakers. Will you teach us?" And
then begin classes with poor attendance. Why? They are busy getting jobs. I am further frustrated by too many phone calls and
counseling visits from women whose problems are compounded by
their working, yet who want me to take time from my family to
solve their problems without even daring to suggest they go *home*
and work there for a change.

I feel guilty even complaining because, as Christians, we are
taught to lift one another's burdens, and I try to do that without
indicating to the one I am helping that it is a burden to me also. I
can do all things with the strength God gives me. But what are
those who may not be Christians saying?

There are many good mothers and homemakers who are not
necessarily Christians who feel infringed upon too.

In February 1981, Lynda G. Parry wrote a letter, "Why Working
Mothers Make Me Mad," for *McCall's* magazine. "As one of the
few remaining members of a nearly extinct species—the full-time

wife and mother—I am worried, frustrated and angry," she says. She is worried because the neighborhood is too quiet now because all the mothers are working and she never hears, "Don't go out without your coat" or, "Come right home after school."

Mrs. Parry can sympathize with working moms who have no choice, and she understands those who need the challenge that working offers. She realizes that she was most fortunate to have the choice, although it was difficult financially. She decided that motherhood should be full time if at all possible, but, she says, "I had no idea my decision would be hampered by the growing number of mothers who work outside their homes."

She feels that the "quality time" mothers tell her they are giving their kids is an overused rationalization. She tries to give hers "quality time" too, but she finds it is the "quantity time" that they thrive on. "Their joys are quick and intense. Their disappointments and defeats don't usually happen during moments set aside for 'quality mothering.'"

Mrs. Parry and her children used to enjoy driving to and from school and other activities. But the intimacy they shared is all but gone as she serves as chauffeur for all the kids of the working mothers. And, Mrs. Parry complained—quite legitimately in my opinion—those mothers were infringing on her "quality time" by allowing their children to arrive too early before school because they didn't like being alone for an hour in an empty house.

And after school they all gather at the Parry's for snacks and play. "It is wearisome always having six to eight children . . . I am tired of cleaning up after all of them." Even when they go home . . .

> the working mothers haven't asked me to be responsible . . . but I feel responsible anyway. I comfort them, discipline them, rescue their pets—or them when they have forgotten their house keys or have locked themselves in the bathroom. I taste batches of peculiar-looking cookie dough, put beserk dishwashers out of their misery and check basements for "funny sounds."[4]

A simple solution to Mrs. Parry's problem and mine as well would be for us to go to work ourselves. But would that really be a solution? The thing that bothers me so much is that much of what God wants us to do—in respect to helping others, caring for the needy and teaching the younger women—flies out the window when we go to work. You can't do everything so you do the best you can at home and at work and that is admirable. But who will do the unpaid work?

Often Proverbs 31 is used in describing the ideal woman. I like that woman because she isn't a dingbat, but an intelligent, capable woman who has her priorities in order. She is busy purchasing everything from wool to fields. She invests in her own ministry of taking care of the needy. She evidently has business sense because she not only makes fine linen but sells it and delivers the goods to merchants. Whether or not she is a public speaker or Sunday School teacher I don't know, but verse 26 says, "She openeth her mouth with wisdom; and in her tongue is the law of kindness."

I like the Proverbs 31 woman most of all because she seems to realize the powerful potential within herself. Verses 27 and 28 show what her priority is in all her important activities *and* her reward: "She looketh well to the ways of her household, and eateth not the bread of idleness. Her children arise up, and call her blessed; her husband also, and he praiseth her."

Like the Proverbs 31 woman, The "keeper at home" cannot be pigeonholed as one type of woman. Rather she is an intelligent manager of the home who maintains the quality of life for those within its walls at the highest level. As diverse as the personalities of the "keepers" are the diversities of homes represented. There is really only one person who can answer the question, "Are you a keeper of your home in a way that is satisfying to the Lord?"

You.

A Prayer from the Keeper

Dear Lord, today I really do feel like a keeper in the zoo. The squeals from the boys swinging from the rope in the tree out back is deafening. The food I keep throwing out to them is running out. I didn't think peanut butter ever ran out.

The hissing from the lioness's den is getting on my nerves, but she had to have that lecture on picking up her clothes. Maybe she will just lick her paws and cool off.

The laundry is piled up and the sound of the hose clues me to the fact I haven't seen anything yet.

The sweat is running down my face and the dust is swirling around on the furniture like tumbleweed in Texas, but I see no need in trying to settle it today.

I would ask You to send them all to some other house to play, but last weekend is still fresh on my mind. You remember all the children were either out of town or spending the night at a friend's, and Marvin was on the West Coast. I reveled in the quiet and I ate what I wanted when I wanted. The house stayed clean for two whole days and I stayed in my robe and typed all day and half the night, but . . . when I was finished with what I wanted to do, I noticed that the house was too quiet, too clean, too uninhabited and too cool. Oh, the house was the same, but those loud, dirty, warm bodies that make it a HOME were surely missed.

Help me remember that, Lord. Amen.

4. The Essence of Home

Somebody has to be the nest maker, the artist, the interior decorator, the imaginative person with a dignity born of understanding its importance . . .

Edith Schaeffer

I love to walk in our neighborhood at night, looking at the houses along the tree hugged streets. Something about seeing the lights in the windows appeals to my imagination. Are families talking over the problems of the day? Are they playing a game? Reading? I know many families are watching TV; the all-too-familiar glow is apparent from the windows. Is their house more than just a place to live? Is it a congenial place where they can retreat from the stressful situations of the impersonal world and enjoy the support of other family members? What is the essence of the home?

Probably all of us have called up images of what our dream home would be like, and if we could compare we might find we share many of the same fantasies. While we might differ on style and layout (my dream *always* has been of a two-story, brick with a winding staircase), we probably see a nice house surrounded by a large, immaculately manicured yard. Very likely there are two handsome cars in the driveway. An entryway filled with fresh flowers and a brightly burning fire in the fireplace beckon you into the living room. Soft, comfortable chairs sitting on clean, thick carpet invite you to sit down and enjoy some relaxed conversation. In my fantasy, candles glow in the dining room, their fragrance mingling with the savory smells from the kitchen where roast beef is browning and spicy apple cake and bran muffins are waiting on the countertop for a festive meal.

Continuing my dream-home fantasy, I think of holidays and people I love. Nestling in the curve of that winding staircase, I see a Christmas tree with laughing children and grownups gathered around, opening brightly colored packages as Christmas carols play softly on the stereo. . . . Love is everywhere. . . .

But the trouble with dreams is the waking up. For a dream to become reality, someone must care enough about it to make it work. This brings us to some important considerations:

1. Is the essence of home as important and valuable that we will sacrifice in order to have it?

2. Who is responsible for maintaining the essence of home?

Caroline Bird, in *The Two-Paycheck Marriage*, foresees a diminishing of value on the dream home.

> Housework will fade away as women give up the dream of home. Our historian grandchildren will be puzzled to read about how their grandmothers struggled to get grandfathers to help with the housework. What housework? Why dress up the bed with traditional spreads and dust ruffles when there will be nobody home to see it all day? Homes won't project the social status of the family. Outsiders won't be able to tell anything about a family or any particular member by finding out where they live, or inspecting their living room furniture.
>
> Eating, too, will be individual. There will still be "family" meals on occasional holidays, but varying schedules will make it hard to get the whole family together for a roast beef dinner or a souffle that can't wait for laggards.
>
> Cooking will survive as a hobby. The business lunch will survive as a ritual.
>
> People will eat whenever or wherever they get hungry.[1]

I don't know how that makes you feel, but it gives me the willies. I may never have all that I dream of, but as long as I live in a free America that dream *is* a possibility. I think it is the dreams that come true that have made this country great. When we cease to dream we will cease to be great.

I believe the essence of a home is important and valuable in God's eyes. And that hopefully gives us incentive to work for it.

Let me paint a picture for you of the first home God prepared for man. He completed it down to the last star-shaped candle before He even invited man to see it.

The scene opens with Genesis 1.

Knowing what chaos and disorder does to the emotions, first God said, "Let there be light." In this He set the clock for man's activity. While it was light he would work, and while it was dark he would rest.

Then God gathered the waters together and called them seas, and He set in motion the rolling tide that would remind man of His constancy and control. On the dry land where man would reside, God planted grasses, herbs, and trees of such variety that man's every whim for color, texture, shape, and taste would be satisfied. This done, He ordered up the accessory lighting to complement the two great chandeliers of sun and moon. These lights, the stars, would serve not only to light man's home but provide for his entertainment and education as well, as he learned much of God's plan for the universe through study of the stars. Knowing that mere "things" would never satisfy the unique, many-faceted personality He intended to invite to this home, God made creatures for the water, air, and land, again of such diversity that man could study their habits forever and never become fully educated. This man would never know boredom.

Against this backdrop of verdant ground studded with bright shapes and sweet smells, canopied with blue, striped with white and bold dashes of yellow and red, God brought his masterpiece, man, to live and move and have his being. Ah, perfect! Adam must have thought at first. But after a while, after examining rough bark and smooth leaves and tasting crunchy nuts and juicy oranges and playing games with his only friends, the animals which he named, he felt something was missing. How could he complain? After all, hadn't his Host thought of everything? What could possibly be missing? Adam certainly couldn't put his finger on it.

I used to wonder why God didn't create man and woman at the same time. Now, I believe He wanted Adam to sense that he wasn't complete and to have a desire for whomever or whatever it was. As Adam examined each wonderful thing he was given, I believe he touched it and smiled and said, "This is beautiful." But I believe that then he sighed, because, after he had touched everything, he knew there must be something else.

God, administering the first general anaesthesia ever, put Adam to sleep. "Son, this little operation will fix you right up." When Adam awoke, God presented him with the gift that completed him—a woman, the female factor.

> And the rib, which the Lord God had taken from man, made he a woman, and brought her unto the man. And Adam said, This is now bone of my bones, flesh of my flesh: she shall be called Woman, because she was taken out of Man (Gen. 2:22–23).

God had pronounced, "It was good," after everything he created, except after he created man. He said, "It is *not* good that the man should be alone; I will make him an helpmeet *for* him." The word *helpmeet* means completer.

The whole of fulfillment, and the answer to what our purpose is, is wrapped up in this passage of Scripture, and in whether we believe it or not.

> Neither was the man created for the woman; but the woman for the man (1 Cor. 11:9).

What is it that gives home its true essence?

It seems clear that none of what God created completed the scene for man's home until He added woman, the female factor. Man is incomplete and unable to fill the purpose God has for his life apart from the completer.

We are back to the principle of cooperating with God in fulfilling the purpose for which He made us.

Of course man could smell the flowers before, but they were more fragrant after the woman came. From the first, man had the potential to run as fast, jump as high, and sing as well as he ever could. But God made him with an ego that needed a cheerleader, and so with the advent of the female factor, he *wanted* to jump higher and run faster.

Once you decide yes, the essence of home is important and I want to keep it—you must also see who is responsible for maintaining the proper balance, the variety, the constancy, the control. God is responsible of course for the "big house" but the female factor came fully equipped to handle the keeping of the home on her level. In fact, the female factor *is* the essence of the home. Remove her and the home is just as incomplete as Adam was before Eve.

Why do men and women avoid going home by stopping at a favorite bar for "happy hour"? Are the atmosphere and conversation more accepting and congenial there than in a setting that seems incomplete? Why do teenagers run away from home at such an alarming rate? Is the home failing to provide the environment where they can find their identity and purpose for life? Is it because the catalyst, who can turn the various sparks and crises into valuable learning experiences, is missing? Is that catalyst the mother?

How valuable is a home compared to just a house or temporary dwelling place? To the redbirds in our backyard, home is the nests built in the tall hedge around our patio. Charlie, the pet squirrel, lives on the third branch in the old oak tree. Why don't birds and squirrels just light wherever they happen to be when their day is over or when they are running from the enemy? Charlie comes to our back door and taps for his daily allotment of crackers and peanut butter. He knows we love him and we would make him a part of our family. But, after he eats, he runs nonstop back to his oak tree abode. Does the familiar home of a nest provide comfort and security for my animal friends?

In the human kingdom we build a variety of nests. For the poor Appalachian coal miner, the old weather-beaten shack on a barren hillside, with its pot-bellied stove blazing, is as comforting as the banker's mansion complete with servants. Why? The old adage "Home is where the heart is" seems to be true, and while we can be fond of our surroundings, our heart usually lies in our relationships with those who share houses with us. Even those who live alone find they have an affection for an old chair that was their dad's or an afghan their grandmother made. Interior furnishings or particular trees and shrubs outside, planted by loved ones, are for many what makes a house a home.

Judging by the number of brides registering for china and silver at the department stores, homes are still being dreamed about. What feeds those dreams?

Certainly, we learn the most from our own mothers about attitudes and values concerning the home. Since television has invaded our homes, we find many women (consciously or unconsciously) patterning themselves after TV's soap opera stars.

One Day at a Time says a single mother raising a teenage daughter can be buddies with her as they share details of their dates. Even though *Soap* was intended as a prime-time spoof of its daytime counterparts, it almost seems to say, for example, that it's all right for the mother in a family to have sex with the butler, the tennis pro, and anyone else interested. The homosexual son is laughed at rather than helped. Various dramas show incestuous relationships, and just recently a miniseries showed two little boys and a little girl investigating each other in a barn. The girl then grew up to be a promiscuous and evil woman. But she was beautiful and she got what she wanted in life, and there may have been young girls watching for whom the so-called "star" of the program became a deceitful role-model. Television has become the most dangerous threat to the family as in show after show it weakens what a home should be. When was the last time you saw a show that depicted the traditional Christian family in a favorable light? Humanism has found a willing vehicle through television.

It is vital that we fight to retain the "essence" of home life. That will vary from family to family, but these special good qualities you have preserved from your own childhood home are valuable and need to be passed down to your own children.

Even with our nifty appliances, it takes much organization and many hours to run our homes smoothly. The time we spend may be as much as our grandmothers spent without modern technology. While we no longer have to scrub on a washboard, we do become

victims of "the repairman wait blues." Shopping today in the maze
of supermarkets, standing in long lines with wallets full of coupons,
takes time. Keeping an upper hand on managing the house, the
clothes, the shopping and the meals is an engineering feat most
men could not handle.

Let's say you are willing to sacrifice all of the time it takes to keep
up the dream. It involves getting children to Boy and Girl Scouts,
soccer and baseball, music and swimming lessons, which can add up
to nearly one full day on the road per week. To keep up the dream,
however, takes more than time; it takes money, lots of money. But
exactly here is a danger point in the American dream, for decisions
are often made that bring about a strange solution—the means
defeats the end. Realizing that the husband isn't able to pay for the
whole dream, but unwilling to scale it down, the female factor goes
to work to make it come true.

The extra money *can* make possible the house, cars, furniture,
the chandeliers and the music lessons. But taking that much time,
effort and emotion to secure the home leaves very little over for
being the "essence."

A friend of mine replied when I asked about going to Washington on a shopping trip, "I can't go because I am working, but if I
wasn't working I couldn't go because I wouldn't have the money."

That is a classic example of what is happening to the home
situation. We have set our dreams too high for the male to achieve
and rather than lower the dream, we go to work to pay for it. Into
their beautiful foyers (with no fresh flowers), women are dragging
bags of groceries, just in time to cook dinner. After dinner, even if
the husband helps his wife with the wash and the dishes, it is too
late to bother with a fire in the fireplace—it would just be one more
thing to clean up. Thanksgiving and Christmas become awful
chores and most women are glad when they are over.

I just heard of a little boy who ran into his house, exclaiming, "I
just love my house; it is the best house in the whole world."

A neighbor who was visiting said "Why don't you visit me? My
house is just like yours, isn't it? What makes yours different?"

"Well, I don't know, I guess it's Mamma!"

Have your dreams of home turned into nightmares? What can you do about it?

1. Evaluate your dream and your motives for having the kind of home you want. Is it pride? Do you want to have a home bigger and better than your friends?

2. Evaluate what it will take to have your dream. Is it worth it? Will it put too much pressure on your husband? Will he have to work another job or will you have to leave the nest to go to work?

3. Evaluate whether or not you would be willing to develop the art of being the "essence" on a smaller scale. You see, being the "essence" means being the life inside the home. You can stay home and keep the fire in the fireplace burning to welcome your world-weary family. That apple spice cake on the counter takes more time than money. Christmas becomes a joyful time of year for all to experience. The pot of beans bubbling on the stove may be much more welcome to your family than a late, hurried dinner of expensive steak.

I guess I take a certain pride in being the essence of my home. Friends have often said, when looking through the various homes we have lived in, "It's you. I could go in every house on this block and I could pick out yours." What do they mean? I have lived in everything from a thirty foot trailer to a brand new home. We now live in a forty-year-old two-story brick—my dream home after twenty-five years. What is me is ruffled curtains and lots of green plants. It is jars of home canned jellies and pickles on open shelves and a pie cooling on the counter. It is still a cradle in the den (for a grandchild now) and a potty chair in the bathroom. It is not sterile neatness, but it *is* happy clutter.

You are the essence of the home just like Eve was the completer for Adam. Are you willing to sacrifice both the time and money in order that this rare, intangible art might be preserved?

When I was twenty-seven-years old I evaluated my life. I added up the physical attractiveness, the good mind, the wonderful family, the material things, and I wondered at my feelings of emptiness. I searched in all the wrong places to find a way to be complete.

In October 1966 I evaluated something else. I was given a little pamphlet by a minister that told me that God loved me and had a plan for my life that included fellowship with Him. It explained that my purpose for being was to have that fellowship but it also told me, "Your iniquities have separated . . . you and your God, and your sins have hid his face from you . . ." (Isa. 59:2, KJV).

It went on to explain that Jesus Christ loved me so much that He was willing to come to earth and die in my place, thus satisfying the demands of God that "the wages of sin is death; but the gift of God is eternal life through Jesus Christ our Lord" (Rom. 6:23).

Not fully understanding how God could love me, but glad He did, I accepted His wonderful offer of salvation through the forgiveness of sins. Jesus Christ moved into my life and my body became His temple. I felt complete for the first time.

We are only complete and content when we are fulfilling that purpose for which we were made. We are loved by the Father, and He longs to have fellowship with us. That is what we were created for. If there is an emptiness in your heart and life as there was in mine, wouldn't you like to invite Jesus Christ to move into your life and give you the "essence" of His life?

No matter what dreams or goals we have set up for ourselves, our families and our homes, if we are not cooperating with God in becoming what He made us for, we will not be content.

Yes, today's women have many choices, but for the Christian woman, the choice is narrowed down to: what is God's will for your life?

Someone recently shared this thought with me: The family is like the Trinity. If the father is likened to God the Father and the children are likened to Jesus the Son, then through the process of elimination, the mother must be likened to the Holy Spirit of the home. For this analogy I looked up some of the attributes of the Holy Spirit, who gives life, teaches, guides, comforts, leads, convicts, and controls. These are just a few, but if the analogy is a good one, we "keepers" get a glimpse of our place in the family. We are not inferior, just as the Holy Spirit is not inferior to the Father or the Son. We just have a different function. Like the Holy Spirit, we won't mind doing the hard work to help the others in the family toward their best. We won't want the attention given to us.

As the Holy Spirit gives life at the new birth, we give life to our children. But even more, we are the life or the "essence" of the home.

Beverly LaHaye, respected for her writing and speaking on the family, puts homemaking at the top of her list of priorities:

> Homemaking is the art of making a home for the members of a family. It is the managing and upkeep of the habitation for loved ones and the providing of an atmosphere of hospitality, warmth, and security. It includes the care and training of the children. The homemaker sets the attitude and environment for all members of the family, including the husband. She contributes to their physical, emotional, mental, and spiritual needs and development.[2]

Mrs. LaHaye says that the emphasis has been placed on the necessary trivia, "as mundane tasks, such as changing diapers, mopping up spilled milk, and doing laundry" rather than the "ultimate goals and final result of shaping human lives that will affect future society." If you are dissatisfied, Mrs. LaHaye says you may be "dwelling on the inconsequential and losing sight of the unselfish, paramount, target."

5. Boom! Another Nuclear Family Just Blew Up!

> *The individual is not truly fulfilled by becoming ever more autonomous. Indeed to move too far in this direction is to risk psychosis—the ultimate form of "autonomy."*
>
> Daniel Yankelovich

*T*he day Marge filed for divorce and Jim moved out it was as if a sudden explosion had ripped through their modest suburban home. The aftermath of the explosion left a confused, frightened little boy of seven sitting on the pile of debris.

"Where will Daddy sleep?" "Who will cook Daddy's dinner?" "Can I still go fishing?" "What if Daddy gets lonesome—can he come back home?"

Marge, a beautiful but determined Superwoman of sorts, had been enlightened by some feminist friends that she didn't have to take it any more.

After long talks with both Marge and Jim, my husband and I gradually learned what "it" was. But "it" wasn't what either Marge and Jim thought it was.

This little family meant a lot to us. We had watched its development from courtship to marriage, to the birth of their son. Their divorce has left a scar on all who know and love them.

Marge rather caustically said, "Don't harp at me about being a working mother. *He* wanted me to work and besides I love my job—it's the one place I am appreciated!"

Marge had a point. After all, she held down an important supervisory job, made as much money as Jim and arrived home later than he on many days. Yet she was expected to prepare the meals, clean the house, keep up with the clothes and all the other things a housewife does. Marge would prepare a huge meal only to have Jim decide he would rather have pizza. He would go to the family room and watch TV and order snacks and drinks as if she were his personal slave.

I told Marge she had a point and I didn't know how she could have done what she did for twelve years with such a sweet attitude. She told me that I missed the point. She didn't mind taking care of all the work and even waiting on Jim, but she just couldn't take the constant criticism and belittling. "He was never satisfied with my performance and was always putting down everything I did."

I believe if they had sought counseling at this point the marriage could have been saved. But the more we talked the more I saw the scraps of trash piled up ready for a fire—discontentment, lack of communication, impatience, negativism and an unforgiving spirit, loss of warmth in physical relationship. Many of us have to deal with our own trash heaps, but before Marge and Jim dealt with theirs, a smoldering ember called "her job" was fanned when she felt appreciated and important at work. This ember caught hold, and with constant fanning of the flame by her feminist friends, a first-class explosion took place. Even five years ago I think Marge would have tried to find a way to save her marriage. Jim really credits the final blow to the "libbers."

In fact, my talk with Jim surprised me. I expected to hear another, dark side of the story that would shock me about Marge. But that wasn't the case. Jim took all the blame: "I wanted to get ahead so badly that I made her work. I know I was too critical of Marge. She seemed to have everything—beauty, brains, a good self-image, a good job—and everyone liked her. I felt so badly about myself; so insecure about my looks, where I stood with her, my job, and all the rest. I know it sounds sick, but I got some satisfaction out of letting her know she wasn't perfect. She did keep a lousy house and was terribly disorganized. She was too lenient on little Jimmy. But the sad thing is, I really love her. We could have worked it out. I would change—she couldn't just sit on a bomb for years and then let it explode without giving me another chance."

Jim further explained that he had neglected her because he was so threatened in his job that he had been going in the office sometimes as early as 6:00 A.M. and coming home as late as 11:00. He felt if he could just be more successful in his career he would feel better about himself. Instead, in one big blast, he lost his home, his wife, and his son.

The Jim and Marge story is duplicated daily hundreds of times—different cities, different names, with slight variations in the script. The bottom line is always the same—*it's over*.

According to the U.S. Census Bureau, the national divorce rate increased 138 percent from 1960 to 1978. Of every 1,000 marriages in the United States, 9.2 ended in divorce in 1960. This number increased to 10.6 in 1965; 14.9 in 1970; 20.3 in 1975, 21.9 in 1978, and continues to climb at a frightening rate.

Destruction of too many marriages results from the partners' uninformed search for individual identity. Before, it was survival of the unit that concerned them; now it is the discovery and protection of the individual. Success in life was equated with the acquisition of homes and material evidence of family affluence. Now the marketplace is flooded with products and services aimed at satisfying the yearning for all kinds of individual self-fulfillment.

Jim and Marge began with the same visions but after twelve years they found that no longer did the gadgets and trappings add up to a home and they experienced their own cultural revolution.

Marge said she failed to *grow* (key word used by self-fulfillment buffs) while married to Jim, that she didn't know who she was and she needed something for herself. She read *Looking Out for No. 1*.

Jim says divorce is worse than a death, because after the funeral, you know that a relationship is finished and you go on. Marital explosions leave lonely men in lonely apartments feeling like failures. Part of a man is blown away when his marriage fails, but part of him will always be in what was once his home.

At first Marge felt euphoric about her new freedoms but now that the dust of her decision has settled, she has begun to have some questions. They don't really involve personal growth of self-actualization but nitty-gritty living: Where are the friends who urged her to get a divorce, thus making a statement about who she was, independent of the male? She wishes one of them would help her cut the lawn, or help her find out why the car is leaking oil. She thought it would be easier to manage things financially with Jim out of the picture. There also were many things she just hadn't thought about at all—things like being frightened in a house all by herself, knowing no one was coming home; of being totally responsible for a fever-wracked little boy in the middle of the night. The friends weren't even there to share in her joy of a promotion. Mainly she had thought of freedom, dating, and fun. Not only did her added responsibilities leave her too exhausted for many dates, but the few she had ended in a "to bed or not to bed" struggle she wasn't ready for. Marge, like many women, is realizing that the expectations of what follows divorce for the working woman had been unreal.

The feminists offered her encounter groups, consciousness-raising and group dynamics, but once her consciousness was raised to the level of knowing how heavy her burdens were, they didn't offer much in the way of concrete sharing of those burdens. She was looking out for No. 1 all right. Alone!

The first time I talked to Marge after the divorce, she said, "I never want to marry again. I can eat what I want, when I want and I plan to date and live and be my own person." The last time I talked to her that inflated "me syndrome" was missing as she said, "The single life is not for me. I miss family life and, believe it or not, I like taking care of a man."

The person most traumatized by the marital explosion is, of course, Jimmy. Children suffer. While I haven't talked to him about it, it's easy to see the pain he feels is sharp. Once when his mommy and daddy were talking on the front lawn before a weekend visit, he tried to put their hands together. As young as he is, he is clearly worried about his future. When his aunt and uncle sent him money for Christmas, he wanted to put it in the bank so he can take care of himself when he grows up. Jimmy is seven.

It was hard for me to believe it when Marge told me how hard Jimmy was to handle, that he wouldn't eat or go to bed. He is not

that way at our house, and I wondered why. I think he likes the
hustle and bustle of a big family, the feuding and fussing, the caring
and teasing. He keeps peeking into the pots simmering on the stove
and eats two helpings of everything. I haven't had the heart to ask
him what hurts the most. I think I know the answer. His mother
works, so she isn't there when he comes home from school, and he
misses his daddy.

The alarming divorce rate (some authorities have estimated this
to be as high as one of every two marriages at the time of this
writing) seems to indicate that couples are not willing to try to stay
together for the sake of children and family. Nor has there been
much inclination on the part of parents to sacrifice individual pursuits and goals in favor of spending more time with their children.
A favorite rationalization talks about "quality time" being more
important than the quantity.

The 1980s White House Conference on Families had difficulty
deciding what a family was. Perhaps this was because participation
was urged from many "self-fulfillment seekers" who had "alternative lifestyles." Do two homosexuals living together constitute a
family? If it becomes legal for two lesbians to adopt a child, will that
constitute a family? The participants finally settled on defining a
family as "all the people living in the same house."

I believe if we put the question to the children of divorce, we
would get the simple but poignant truth—mother, father and children. I know that it is not always possible to have that structure and
that some marriages are so painful that struggling alone seems uto-
pian by comparison.

But, just how important is the traditional family?

The Book of Knowledge says that a family is the most important
group to which most people ever belong and that it does many
things such as caring for daily needs of its members. It says that
members find love, sympathy, and companionship more easily than
in any other group. [1]

However, Caroline Bird predicts that all of this is changing:

Family members won't tackle each other's emotional problems.
They'll be handled by professionals or support groups of others who are

coping with them. We've learned that heavy drinkers can get more help from a pickup "family" of fellow alcoholics than almost anyone else.

Families will get along better with each other because they will depend on each other primarily as friends. There will be less chance to quarrel over money, behavior, possessions, manners, or each other because neither parents nor children nor husbands nor wives will be each others' only source of emotional support. Families will spend less time with each other.[2]

During the past few years the term *nuclear family* has come into existence. Just thinking of *nuclear* as it relates to atomic energy and weapons, my mind conjured up the thought of the nuclear family as being explosive. It seems an apt description of nearly 50 percent of today's families. In asking *why*, I could not get away from the implications of the female factor as it relates to the family.

The word *nuclear* is derived from *nucleus*, meaning "a central thing or part around which other things are grouped." It also means "center of growth or development." Is it too bold to suggest that the female factor is the nucleus of the family?

In the following diagram I have drawn what I consider a picture of the family. If God ordained the family, His characteristic order, structure, and wisdom of pattern must be evident.

THE NUCLEAR FAMILY

The comforting truth that we each have an outer rim of comfort, protection and strength to lean on, provides what we need to have a strong Christian family. What emanates from the nucleus, love, gentleness, goodness, longsuffering, meekness, and strong moral convictions actually comes from Christ living in the female factor (Col. 1:27). It flows all the way through the family, through children, husband until it reaches back to the outer rim or the Source—God. As the female factor connects with the outer rim again, she is infused with more of His nature and quality and it flows back through the family.

One woman asked me, "Why should all that responsibility be on

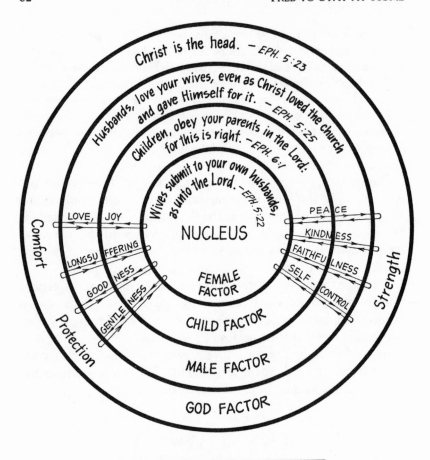

Christ is the head. – EPH. 5:23

Husbands, love your wives, even as Christ loved the church and gave Himself for it. – EPH. 5:25

Children, obey your parents in the Lord: for this is right. – EPH. 6:1

Wives submit to your own husbands, as unto the Lord. – EPH. 5:22

NUCLEUS

FEMALE FACTOR

CHILD FACTOR

MALE FACTOR

GOD FACTOR

LOVE, JOY

LONGSUFFERING

GOOD NESS

GENTLE NESS

PEACE

KINDNESS

FAITHFULNESS

SELF-CONTROL

Comfort

Protection

Strength

THE NUCLEAR FAMILY

my back?" I don't know the answer to that. I just know when the Father offered the bitter cup to His Son, Jesus said, "Not my will, but thine be done."

God has a design, a plan for life, and as I see it I have a very important place in that plan. Sometimes the cup looks bitter for me too, but I try to say, "Not my will, but thine." The bottom line to the true fulfillment issue is *obedience*, cooperating with God in being what He made me to be.

Larry Christenson says that "in the Christian family, on a small scale, should be seen the wisdom and gentleness of command, the willingness of obedience, the unity and firmness of mutual confidence which will characterize the perfected kingdom of God.[3]* Ephesians 5:21—6:4 lays out this principle.

If the family as we know it is to be destroyed, the nucleus must be weakened. Men have gone off and left their families since the beginning of time, and while this is inexcusable, and has brought suffering and hardship to the family, it doesn't necessarily destroy the unit. A Christian mother who loses the outer rim of emotional, physical, and spiritual support provided by the male factor, can, by leaning more on the God factor, still provide the proper home for her children. But the female factor who vacates her position as nucleus leaves a void that cannot be filled. No other can meet the needs of her family as well as she can.

I didn't fully realize the importance of my role as center of the family until I started researching for this book. During our younger years, when it is perhaps most important for our families, we are inclined to be the most obtuse. I am convinced that is why it is God's design that the older women teach the younger. It seems that in our early family life, we don't understand our own vital contribution to the total well-being of family members. Many younger women tell me they can't find fulfillment in being "just a housewife." Perhaps we need to ask ourselves what we mean by "being fulfilled." How do *you* define fulfillment?

I don't know the answers to all those questions but if you are facing an explosion at your house you might consider trying to answer them yourself.

An article appearing in April 1981 in *Psychology Today*, "New Rules in American Life: Searching for Self-Fulfillment in a World Turned Upside Down," is the culmination of four years of work by Daniel Yankelovich. Yankelovich, who is president of the social research firm of Yankelovich, Skelly, and White, Inc., has been research professor of psychology at New York University and a

---

*Reprinted by permission from *The Christian Family* by Larry Christenson, published and copyright 1970, Bethany Fellowship, Inc., Minneapolis, Minnesota 55438.

visiting professor of psychology at the graduate faculty of the New School for Social Research.

This secular article, backed up by surveys, research, and impressive statistics, paints in broad strokes the picture of where our society and culture are headed if we continue our mad search for self-fulfillment. Yankelovich reported that their studies showed nearly 80 percent of the population to be engaged in the search for self-fulfillment. Further, he said, research data indicates that our future is being shaped by cultural revolution in which we seem to have discarded those values and meanings that our forebears pursued with such fervor.

In place of the pattern of commitment and self-sacrifice in family living, "doing your own thing" has become the norm—fulfillment of the individual without regard to the effect on personal relationships, even the very closest ones. But the pendulum is swinging back. Magazines and newspapers, TV and radio talk-shows report and discuss a growing desire for a return to the family way of life.

Why do we as Christians look to "worldly" sources for our solutions to life's problems? We become as confused by the "self" psychology as non-Christians as we search for answers in books with titles like How to Be Your Own Best Friend, Pulling Your Own Strings, and Looking Out for No. 1.

One day the authors of the above books are being touted as the discoverers of real fulfillment on your local talk show on TV. A few years later another psychologist-author exposes the theories as "moral and social absurdity." In the meantime, how many are left floundering and directionless, their family life decaying as it is affected by an inward decay on a personal level?

What then is self-fulfillment? Of course I can't answer that for anyone else. But I am sure of one thing—true fulfillment will never negate what God has ordained and declared to be good. If your idea of pursuing "duty-to-self" involves anything that is a threat to your family, directly or indirectly, I suggest you may need to seek not self-fulfillment but God's will for your life.

I would describe fulfillment as being in the place God wants me to be and enjoying it. Contentment equals fulfillment. This feeling is mine when I prepare a great meal for my family or arrange a room beautifully for them to enjoy or even hold a sick child through the night. My greatest fulfillment is just beginning to be realized as I view my children from afar and see them succeeding in life as responsible, productive, stable, caring individuals who will make the world a better place. Sound trite? . . . Maybe, but ask yourself some questions:

1. Why am I working?
2. What would happen if I didn't work?
3. How would the family suffer if I stopped working?
4. How would the family benefit if I were to be a full-time keeper of the home?

In light of your answers to these questions—and I suggest you write these answers out so you can actually see and evaluate them—what have you learned about your priorities and values?

Looking back at Marge and Jim, whom we met at the beginning of this chapter, what positive factors might have saved their marriage? Would the couple have been able to meet each other's emotional needs better had Marge had more time and energy to devote to it? If Marge hadn't been "shown" that she was "unfulfilled," would she have known or felt it? Was "time" an important enemy? Marge said she couldn't grow and do things that would bring her personal fulfillment because all she had time for was work and home. Would she have been better off to sacrifice her job and the salary rather than her family?

Jim Elliott, seven years before his death as a missionary, said: "He is no fool who gives what he cannot keep to gain what he cannot lose."[4] Jesus Christ himself said: "For whosoever will save his life shall lose it; and whosoever will lose his life for my sake shall find it" (Matt. 16:25). This chapter began with reference to the "nuclear" family. Every country that understands that no one actually can win in a nuclear holocaust, spends enormous amounts of time, energy, and money in preventing such an occurrence. The female factor must also spend energy and time in preventing attack on her family. But her secret, most powerful weapon is not the stockpiling of more and more means of destruction; rather, it is self-denial and sacrifice.

6. Falling in Love Again

> Many marriages fail because couples cease to be
> sweethearts.
>
> Marie Corelli

While speaking to Christian Women's Clubs recently in central Virginia I was thoroughly charmed by the darling, dark-haired young woman who presented the secular portion of the program. The representative of a major airline, she was demonstrating the correct way to pack luggage. Her sparkling humor kept everyone in stitches as she wove cute stories in with the practical techniques.

Since we were both on the program for four clubs, I learned how to pack with a chuckle and she learned my story of victory over trials. She read my book, *Dear Mamma, Please Don't Die,* between the first and second day, and we spent some time talking about living the Christian life. She admitted that while she was a Christian, she had not really made Christ Lord of her life.

Right before we were to part company she asked to speak to me. "Marilee, I have a problem I don't quite know how to solve. I'm married to a very handsome, fun-loving man who obviously loves me, and we have one teenage son. My husband just accepted a move to Houston where he has purchased a beautiful home and a membership in a country club. He's waiting for me to move down. My problem is twofold: (1) I love my job and have a chance for advancement here; and (2) I don't think I love my husband any more and I don't want to move.

"I have already seen a psychiatrist and he told me to hold onto my handsome husband and the home and country club membership but to have an affair. I don't think that's what I need, is it?"

Practicing the art of never looking shocked, I sent my S.O.S. up to the Lord. "O.K., Lord, what can I say to this gorgeous creature who obviously can take care of herself?" I took my cue from, "I love my job."

Reaching for her hand and smiling, I said, "Oh, you are so wise in realizing that an affair is not what you need. Have you ever thought of falling in love again with your own husband?"

Her troubled face clearly registered surprise. "What do you mean?"

"I won't deny that an affair would be exciting and bring back some good feelings. You and your lover would probably spend time on the phone and over dinner finding out what is important to each other. You would put extra care into how you looked for him and what you said. You would most likely buy him gifts and prepare special meals. But, if you were to put that extra thought, effort, money, and time into finding out about the man wrapped up in your husband, you might just find yourself falling in love again. I would guess that you know only about 20 percent of what you can learn about him. What if you give him up and some other woman discovers the remaining 80 percent and you then really admire what she discovers?

"You have several important things going for you that most women are searching for: (a) he loves you; (b) he is willing for commitment; (c) he willingly sacrifices for you and works hard to provide you with a wonderful life. He is willing to go out on a financial limb because making you happy is his goal. Not many men want that today.

"Consider, too, the effect divorce or an affair would have on your son. Then ask yourself: Am I willing to sacrifice a job that offers me temporary fulfillment in independent finances and excitement for a lifetime relationship that demands self-denial and sacrifice on both our parts?"

Later, seated comfortably in a coffee shop, we were eating scrambled eggs and toast and discussing some principles that seemed to be working in my marriage.

"You know, Kate, in order to have scrambled eggs, you have several definite factors. You *must* have eggs and heat, and in order to make the blending, you need a fork or spoon to stir. There are other factors that are variables. A pan is nice, but you could scramble eggs on a hot sidewalk. You can spice them up, have them firm or soft, or even make an omelet with cheese and onions. There are all kinds of possibilities once you have the eggs and the heat. The end result is determined by what you put into it.

"So it is with marriage. You begin with the male and female factors, but it is the third factor that stirs and blends the two, and that is love. Millions of words have been written trying to describe love but it is still a mystery. God is a unique chemist. He alone can bring the real love factor into operation with the right male and female factor. Once He does, He makes all things possible but He leaves that up to the cooks. The spice of your marriage depends upon what you put into it. Whether it is hot or cold, interesting or boring is not up to the chemist but up to you."

Departing from that analogy, I explained that marriage *does* have life in it. And like any other living thing, marriage must face its winter seasons when all looks grey and dead and feels cold; its seed time and harvest. Surviving the winters is often the toughest time for many in marriage, and it's during these frigid periods that many of them die. Many are suffering from a hopelessness that there will ever be a new springtime.

After a brittle, grey February in Virginia, I keep an eye on the hard ground where my tulip bulbs are buried and I watch the tiny nubs on bare trees in anticipation of a fruitful spring. Don't just wait for spring in your marriage; *look* for signs and rejoice when you see them. And don't compare your marriage with anyone else's, because just as winter lasts longer in the north, every marriage has its own timetable. Even marriages that were once blooming and fertile sometimes seem doomed and sterile. We laugh at the seven-year itch and cry at the midlife crisis, but marriage can suffer an Arctic winter at any time—after the birth of a child or during a husband's preoccupation with career or when the children are all gone. Whatever the reasons, when the cold north wind begins to blow over your marriage, you need to go to your mental attic and drag out some extra quilts to see you through. But you *can* get through.

Perhaps it's attitude that needs working on. Maybe you've been too lazy to spice up your marriage and prevent it from becoming bland and boring. Could it be that you're frozen because you haven't thrown the quilt of forgiveness over hurt feelings or temporary neglect? Thawing not only feels good, but it is vital to new growth and cleansing and refreshing.

I don't know how you met and fell in love—we all have different circumstances and our own private "love story." Some are ecstatic "love-at-first-sight" stories while others may reflect a slow growing in love, and some are even humorous. That doesn't matter now, except that you may need to try and recall the feelings and emotions for a frame of reference with which to begin.

Many women I talk to who feel trapped in a bad marriage have a *mental offense list.* To hear them tell it, there was nothing good about their mates. I always ask them why they were so dumb as to marry such a brute. That gets a raised eyebrow or two! With so many women scared about marriage and motherhood, many are taking too long to count the cost. At the same time, I agree that more thought needs to go into such a commitment than many of us gave.

"He wasn't like this when we met. He has changed."

"In what way?" I ask.

The standard answers are:

1. He was so romantic—where did that go?

2. We never tired of talking to each other—now we just grunt when we need to communicate.

3. We used to have so much in common.

I don't doubt that your husband has changed, but haven't you?

What do you do to keep the fires of romance from going out in the bedroom of your marriage? Have you sent a message that he is

not important enough to keep yourself beautiful for? When my
husband married me I was just a girl, and now twenty-five years
later I am still *his girl.* It's his girl he takes out and not the mother of
his children. And he certainly doesn't think of himself taking a
grandmother to bed.

Almost everything about me has changed—looks, attitudes,
and values. One of the main reasons I take the time and trouble to
diet, exercise, and dress attractively is that I believe the female
factor is the one who carries in the logs for the fire of romance by
setting the mood, dressing the part, and having the correct mental
attitude.

Like most brides, I thought our love was big enough to see us
through anything. I believed my mate loved me enough to overlook
a steady decrease in personal protection of my femininity and attractiveness and a slow but steady increase in dress size.

Indeed, he has loved me through a couple of ugly seasons, like
staying with me during multiple sclerosis when statistics show that
most mates leave. However, I don't think that is worthy of a gold
button, because our wedding vows said, "in sickness and in
health." We have survived periods of emotional drought and psychological adjustment, and we don't deserve an Oscar for that
either because of the "for better or worse" clause. But, emerging
from those seasons, I realized I wanted to bestow my own private
award. It wasn't that I just felt I owed him, but I had a desperate
need to show him my deep gratitude by giving him the best I had—
body, soul, and spirit. That involves a creative conscience commitment to keeping the romance alive.

Ann Landers printed a letter over twenty years ago that I
heeded. It came from a woman who was lonely and jealous of the
time her husband spent at a local diner. Ann said, "When you
begin to offer the same thing on the menu at home, he may spend
his time there."

It does take two to tango, but someone must ask first, "Would
you care to dance?" A creative female factor will dare to seek ways
for stoking the fire.

Lack of communication is a problem in even the best of marriages because in the beginning you are busy discovering everything

about each other—but that can only take so long. Many couples who spent hours together on the phone and in front of the fireplace find themselves silently consuming their favorite meals without a word of gratitude or even small talk.

In the early days of marriage the female factor can set the stage for lifelong verbal sharing by kindly expressing how much it means to her to have a compliment on her meals, her appearance, her domestic abilities, and her role as a mother. True romance begins in the mind, is initiated through words of love, and culminates in the act of love.

The male factor needs ego-building more in other areas: his masculinity, his body, his professional abilities, and his performance toward his family.

Don't just talk about clogged garbage disposals and the traffic en route to the orthodontist. Talk about feelings, dreams, disappointments—pump the bellows rather than throwing onto the fire damp, green wood that won't catch and burn.

Communication is more than verbal. Touching, rubbing shoulders, and softly holding hands say, "I love you so much that I must touch you." Eye language, that secret code, transmits a message across a crowded room, "I'm thinking warm thoughts about you."

While it usually takes communication to lead to romance, during the white heat of early romance a unique thing occurs. The two opposites that nearly always attract each other as a fly is drawn to flypaper are so anxious to please that she says things like, "Oh yes, I just love football," or he crosses his fingers and says, "I love opera too."

I don't know why we are so shocked to find that with the relaxation that envelops a marriage, the real persons emerge. When Marvin and I dated, I would snuggle next to him in the car and smile and look like I *loved* country music. I *did* wait until after the honeymoon to tell what I really thought about it.

Couples will split up over grievances caused by this phenomenon of "we have nothing in common." Then each searches for another and marries, only to find the same thing.

It is best to know very early that we may not have much in common but to help each other over the weaknesses and to enjoy the "double portion of strengths." The differences in the male and female are so vast, I can't understand why we would even *think* we had much in common.

I explained to Kate that when I first became a Christian, I didn't have anyone to teach me any practical things about the "keeping" of a marriage other than submission. I would ask, "Is submission all there is?" The lessons were almost always from Ephesians 5.

One Sunday our Sunday School teacher was teaching on this passage and my ears jumped to attention at some of the things he said. One was that we were to mutually surrender to each other and that this actually meant becoming addicted to each other. He explained that it is the commitment that leads to addiction.

The teacher also explained that marriage love, unlike any other, calls for all three levels of love, as expressed in the Greek terms for them.

1. *Eros.* Most marriages begin with this emotional, passionate love that is physical in nature, involving sexual excitement. Our word *erotic* comes from *eros.*

2. *Phileo.* This is the companionship love. It means brotherly friendship and is vital to a marriage.

3. *Agape.* This is divine love that, unlike the other two, does not depend on a response. This love is not limited to circumstances nor is it conditional. We must draw on this love from the only source available, God.

Using that discussion as a springboard, with the help of my husband, I developed five things that I believe a husband wants in a wife. If you desire, as I do, to be the best wife possible, you won't be shocked by the demand for these multiple personalities needed in a marriage.

1. *Merry Mistress.* The female factor can spark up a dull marriage with a new cookbook and a new nightie. Those are two basic biological needs that a man wants to have filled, but most men *seek* a sexual partner and *hope* she can cook. The truth is, if wives were satisfying their needs men wouldn't seek mistresses. You may have to fantasize a bit to try to figure what a mistress does, but I don't think that will take long. A mistress just plans for, and works at,

satisfying a man sexually. A Christian woman must discard the idea that enjoying sex is wrong.

> God's design for women goes beyond roles of wife, mother, and companion. It includes her being a lover—a sexual partner in marriage—enjoying herself and experiencing pleasure. God, the Creator of sex, set human drives in motion not to torture men and women, but to bring them to completion and fulfillment.[1]

One thing a mistress knows is the difference between the sexes.

> Radical feminists have vocally denounced other sexual differences and have declared that any distinction between the sexes is culturally and environmentally inspired. Dr. James Dobson strongly opposes this mistaken idea and states that males and females differ biochemically, anatomically, and emotionally. . . . Men carry different chromosomal patterns than women. The emotional center provides women with a different psychological basis than men. Female sexual desire tends to be cyclical, while the sex drive in males is acyclical. Men are stimulated visually, and women are stimulated by the sense of touch. Sex for a woman is usually a deeply emotional experience, culminating in a feeling of warmth and affection. For men, it is strongly physical, leaving them exhausted and sleepy.[2]

What a man likes in a mistress is that she doesn't bother him about Suzie's bad grades, a leaky faucet, or the need for storm windows when he is in the mood for love. Granted, she is not responsible for those things, but let's take a lesson from her about timing. One young man remarked about a night when romance was stopped dead at the moment his wife said, "The ceiling needs painting."

I am not, to my knowledge, acquainted with any mistresses, but I can almost guarantee that they don't wear a torn flannel nightgown and a chenille robe pinned at the neck with a big safety pin. Someone is wearing those flimsy, lacy nighties I see in such a profusion of styles, colors, and prices in department stores.

Yes, a man wants a Merry Mistress, one who is an eager participant in the love act and who is anxious to please her partner. Merry means "full of fun and laughter; lively and cheerful; gay, mirthful, festive and amusing," according to Webster. Of course, I know some men are selfish, insensitive brutes when it comes to sex. In *The Husband Book* Dean Merrill says:

> The point is that sex is a joint dimension in which both husbands and wives give pleasure to each other, thereby communicating their love in a largely nonverbal way. It is an experience in giving. It is another situation for being the servants of our wives. In fact, it may be one of the more difficult situations in which we are called upon to serve, given our Western macho traditions of sexual conquest. From boyhood on, we men have been programmed in a thousand different ways to view sex as an area where we *get*, where we *take*, where we *use*. The culture is thoroughly saturated with the image of Don Juan.[3]

Mr. Merrill goes on to say that the way some men enjoy sex with their wives is just short of rape. In cases of severe sexual problems and especially in abuse cases, counseling needs to be sought. According to an article in the May 1981 *Ladies' Home Journal*, the type of counseling is very important. The article, written by Barbara Harris, "Let's Bring Love Back to Sex" exposes the so-called sex therapy of Masters and Johnson and others, as promoting the learning of a repertoire of sexual techniques rather than helping couples improve the quality of their life together through "lovemaking."

Since I am basically a very modest person, it would be very artificial for me to come on like Marabel Morgan. I get the same results by being fresh and feminine and responding warmly. Most men don't need trench coats, hip boots and whips to stimulate them, unless they are comatose. What they need is the sight of femininity, the smell of sweetness, the touch of softness and a quick, eager response. I have yet to hear of a man who is turned on by a masculine woman. If a man whistles at a woman in fatigues, you can be sure it is because of the way she fills them out.

Try to wear gowns and perfumes that say "I'm in the mood for love." Comb your hair, leave off the grease and wear a little lipstick to bed. Keep the bedroom as attractive and pleasant as possible. We try to slip away together every so often on a date, overnight, where we have time to really listen to each other without the negative distractions of home (phone, etc.) and can concentrate on love. The act of love is a thermometer that gauges the temperature of the marriage. If there are buried angers or hostilities, it is most difficult to participate eagerly. This is why it is so important to communicate constantly. However, the warmth and joy of the love act can actually wash away minor hurts and neglects that may grow out of proportion otherwise.

What affect does the wife's working have on sex? Caroline Bird says:

> Most couples who think that sex is changed when a wife goes to work tend to say that it is changed for the worse. They're too tired, too tense, or their schedules conflict. Many people believe that the tension of professional and business life can cut into sex.
>
> Hard-working professional women are too tense themselves to help their husbands relax enough so that sex is good for them both. "It's hard to be in the mood for sex when both of us are scratching as hard as we can to get some sort of edge over the competition," a Contemporary Wife told us. "I'll bet a lot of couples aren't telling their friends that they aren't sleeping with their husbands."[4]

2. *Fast Friend.* More and more in our troubled world we find ourselves misunderstood and hurt. Whether men talk about it as much as women is debatable. But one thing is not debatable—a man wants his wife to be his friend. Recently I read of a study of 1500 marriages citing as the number one complaint of men was that wives talk too much and don't listen enough.

> When women spend more time with each other, and with their work, men feel the desertion keenly. It is worse now than in the past, Goode asserts, because they are more dependent on women for solace and intimacy than they were when there were more all-male organizations and clubs than there are now.[5]

The pattern in adulterous triangles: The unfaithful husband didn't start out to be unfaithful—he first became interested in the other woman because she was so *understanding*. (Sound familiar?) It

wasn't a physical, sexual thing at first. It was simply that she wanted to listen to him and his wife never did. It started as warm
companionship and somewhere it got out of hand.

While friendships of the same sex are very important, I realized
some time ago that if I put the time, money, and effort into building a friendship with my husband I would have a friend that
wouldn't move away, didn't take gas to visit, and, in my case,
would pay for his own presents. More and more we both realize that
we would just as soon be with each other than anyone we can think
of.

3. *Secret Saver.* While man's physical needs are great his emotional needs may even outweigh them. A man needs one person to
whom he can be completely open without fear of judgment, with
whom he can share his weaknesses without being made to feel
weak. He needs a person he can try out his dreams on without fear
of dream-smashing. Proverbs 31 speaks of the woman whose husband "doth safely trust in her." One wonders, with the current
status of impermanent live-in relationships, just who trusts whom
with what. Both the man and the woman need to be able to trust
each other with their most intimate feelings and private secrets.

While most women wouldn't consider being physically intimate
with another woman, they do share their other intimacies with
other women, and some men are jealous of that.

4. *Mood Monitor.* Being able to sense your mate's mood and
adapting to it is not easy but is a gift most men, if not all, want in
their wives. When you sense he has been trounced on all day in the
business world, you know it is not the ideal time to tell him where
he is also failing at home. When his ego is ailing, you know it is the
right time for admiration and appreciation for the things he *does
right.* When he is enjoying a high achievement period and his ego is
big as all outdoors, you will have a better climate for dealing with
other problem areas. Programming your heart, mind, and mouth so
that the feedout properly coincides with his mood will create a
climate conducive to happy personal growth in a marriage. A wife
can and should be her husband's best cheerleader and morale boost-
er. The effort often comes back doublefold.

A man who constantly berates his wife and criticizes her every move is a man who feels terrible about himself. My early dislike of myself led me to be Marvin's chief dream-smasher. We all have a right to our dreams and, while I know they might not come true, I appreciate being let in on them. Who knows, they might come true.

5. *Homemaker.* Whether or not a woman works outside the home, most men want their wives to be in control of the home. They really *do* want a castle to come home to.

> Careful time studies show that while husbands may help a little with a long list of tasks, they are not serious, committed homemakers. The husbands studied by Kathryn Walker of Cornell averaged no more than 1.6 hours of household work a day, and the Michigan husbands helped only a few hours a week. According to a study of time use sponsored by the United Nations, husbands are much the same all over the world.[6]

I have long believed that the female factor has it 100 percent over the male in terms of what it takes to put together an enjoyable, comfortable, workable home. It may be that you are full time at running a home successfully; or maybe part-time or even managing to have the outside help of a housekeeper, maid, or cleaning lady periodically. However you do it, keeping the home is basically the woman's task, and it needs to be done as unto the Lord.

It sounds incredibly old-fashioned, but I feel that a man should come home without having to worry about what's for dinner or whether or not he has a clean shirt. I know the women's libbers are demanding, "Who cares what *I* have for dinner and who is going to wash *my* shirt?" Believe me, I *do* know how they feel. Sometimes I get fed up with taking care of everyone, but then I remember that possibly my husband gets a bit weary with paying our bills and having so much responsibility every day!

> Homemakers can plan their work so that they are available to spend leisure time with their husbands and children in the evening and on weekends. The Michigan time-use studies show that working women use this "leisure" time to do the chores that homemakers get done while they are at home alone. "I see too many people working so hard that

they can't enjoy life," a Traditional Wife explained as her reason for
staying at home. "I feel we are happier than most."

Working or nonworking, a wife is responsible for the family lifestyle.
The working wives never got a chance to relax.[7]

According to Ms. Bird, (most) men are willing to do varying
degrees of housework and some men actually enjoy doing certain
tasks. That is great. Every couple is unique and what works for you
is wonderful. But, I believe some women who are so unhappy
handling the homefront need to analyze what their husbands *do*
contribute. Furthermore, I love to cook and keep house and I know
women who hate it, for whatever reason. I'm not saying they are
wrong or failing; I'm just saying, work hard at finding a solution
between the two of you before the problem becomes a wedge driving you apart.

A woman who was recently divorced after nine years, because
"He still hadn't changed," asked me, "To what do you attribute
your long marriage? Is it based on sex, need, or what?" My answer
was quick: "I guess it's because I married my best friend." I went
home thinking about that, and I discovered that it is not so much
what my marriage *is* based on but what it *is not* based on that is
making it work.

You may recognize some of the terms in the list that follows.
These are some of the north winds that have put a chill on our
marriage from time to time. We *are not* letting them into our hearts
now. If you are asking, "How can I fall in love again, when I
have been hurt so often?" you might try some of the quilts I suggest.
They have been known to thaw out frosty marriages.

1. *Selfishness.* Philippians 2:21 says, "For all seek their own, not
the things which are Jesus Christ's." I have opened the door to the
frosty blast more than once by insisting on having my own way. I
don't know a person alive who doesn't want his or her own way.
But I do know some who are controlled by the Holy Spirit and are
able to bow to the desires of another because of it.

Philippians 2:2–5 gives the quilt you need to snuggle under to
keep warm. It is a beautiful quilt with patterns and designs—not a
crazy quilt. It takes many tedious stitches and many hours to put it
together, but it's worth it.

Fulfill ye my joy, that ye be like-minded, having the same love, being of one accord, of one mind. Let nothing be done through strife or vainglory; but in lowliness of mind let each esteem other better than themselves. Look not every man on his own things, but every man also on the things of others. Let this mind be in you, which was also in Christ Jesus.

I can hear that! You just said, "Why should I always give in? Why should he get his way all the time?" I understand how you feel and I'm surely not saying it is always fair, but I am saying it is possible by inviting the Holy Spirit to control your life. In fact, not only can it be painless but just come naturally because that's how the Holy Spirit is. For, you see, in verse seven of that same chapter, Jesus is said to have "made himself of no reputation, and took upon him the form of a servant. . . ."

2. *Self-hatred.* If you are finding it hard to love your mate as you feel you should, you may need to examine how you feel about yourself. Sometimes unknowingly we carry into marriage something our partner didn't bargain for, a feeling of low self-worth. Wherever we received that training—in childhood or later—we have to learn to love ourselves before we can properly love another. Psalm 139:14 says, "I will praise thee; for I am fearfully and wonderfully made. . . ." God did not make a mistake when designing you.

Some things I hated about me that I now rather like: (a) My height—when all the cute girls in high schools seemed to be 5'2" I hated my 5'6½". Now that I constantly battle with fifteen to twenty pounds of excess weight I am much better off than my counterpart. She has to show what I can sometimes hide under a blazer. (b) Of more serious consequence, I hated my melancholy temperament. I wanted so to be like my exuberant, outgoing husband who saw a rainbow in every sky while I concentrated on the black clouds. When I realized after the self-mortification of an attempted suicide that even God wouldn't allow me to stamp our the real Marilee Horton, I took another look. I was surprised to find out that God needs people like me too. If I hadn't been so low, how could I say to a weary pilgrim, I know, I know? If I hadn't seen the Lord could lift my head up, how could I say, this too shall pass, this bitter cup!

I didn't need my temperament, personality, and character stamped out—only controlled.

3. *Anger and bitterness.* Not many couples go through marriage without ever becoming angry. If they do, perhaps they should be writing this book.

Shortly after you say "I do," you *do* begin to see things you didn't know were there while you romanced in the moonlight. Things like soppy wet towels and clothes on the floor and loud snores rocking you from the bed, moody spells and silence. The natural reaction is anger. But Christians are not to be natural but super-natural. Anger not dealt with will turn into the full-blown bitterness warned about in Hebrews 12:15: "Looking diligently lest any man fail of the grace of God; lest any root of bitterness springing up trouble you, and thereby many be defiled."

The quilt needed to cover these drafty places in your marriage is a strange one, just one pattern of three parts repeated over and over again. (a) Face anger as a sin (Eph. 4:30–32). To justify or excuse our anger defeats us in the long run. (b) Confess your anger to God (1 John 1:9). The word *confess* means to own up to or admit. I believe we need to verbally admit to God that we did what we did and that we want help in not doing it again. (c) Ask God to take away the habit pattern (1 John 5:14, 15). The moment we confess we are forgiven and cleansed and the moment we ask to be filled with the Spirit we must believe that we are. Only through consistent walking in the Spirit will we gain control over this marriage-destroying habit.

I like to picture the "grace of God" mentioned in the above verse as the spool of thread needed to make this quilt. As long as we pull from the spool, we have thread for the job. It is up to us, and we can stop pulling any time we want. So it is with God's grace. He longs to supply all the grace we will ever need to keep us sweet and free from bitterness. All He asks is that we receive it and not stop the flow.

4. *Infidelity:* I guess there is nothing that will hang icicles on the marriage like unfaithfulness. While I have heard every excuse in the book and nearly fallen for some, there *is* no excuse for unfaithfulness. There is nothing as comforting as the wedding-ring

quilt. Each ring is intertwined with another and each stands for a year of marriage. For any one of those rings to be broken would spoil the beauty of the quilt. However, there is a second quilt to be used if that happens. This quilt is made up of letters spelling *forgiveness*. "Forbearing one another, and forgiving one another, if any may have a quarrel against any: even as Christ forgave you, so also do ye" (Col. 3:13). Strangely enough, the underside of this quilt is inscribed with a verse that will teach you what you are to do if you are tempted to be unfaithful, it reads: "Mortify therefore your members which are upon the earth; fornication, uncleanness, inordinate affection, evil concupiscence, and covetousness, which is idolatry" (Col. 3:5).

How do you mortify the desire to be with another man? You must kill the desire like you would kill the desire to drink. Starve it! It would be difficult to kill the appetite for alcohol if you spent most of your time in a bar or looking at pictures of or dreaming of a tall, cool drink. You have to replace these images with others. In the same way, you can't break the desire to be with another while still seeing him or day-dreaming about him. Why do most women say they can't kill the desire? I believe they don't want to. If that is your case, I would ask you to pray that our Father would then at least give you the desire to do the right thing.

5. *Emotional disorders.* While your mate may long to be the best partner and love you with all his heart, if you fall prey to anxiety attacks, worry-wartiness, free-floating fears and dreary depressions, he may find it hard to keep the love fires burning. I have been a victim to all of the above, and I don't know of an uglier period in my life. When I got to the root of these problems, they pointed to a lack of trust in my Creator, but as far as my husband could see, I was saying to him: I don't believe you can or will take good care of the family. I don't trust you.

In this case I didn't need a quilt or a blanket to share with another; rather, I needed my own personal robe—a robe made up of many colors and many verses from the word of God. The fear, worry, anxiety, and depression I had was real to me even if no one else could understand it. In other words, it wasn't a family problem but mine alone. I wanted to be a whole, normal, healthy person, and the Lord showed me in John 15:7, "If ye abide in me, and my words abide in you, ye shall ask what ye will, and it shall be done unto you." I asked to be whole and He told me what to do. It was that simple and I began searching the Bible for verses to apply to my life. The verses were woven together to make up the robe that now covers my wounds so well I hardly remember them.

For help with *anxiety* and *fear:*

> Be careful (or fearful) for nothing; but in every thing by prayer and supplication with thanksgiving let your requests be made known unto God. And the peace of God, which passeth all understanding, shall keep your hearts and minds through Christ Jesus (Phil. 4:6–7).

For help with *depression,* recognizing that depression is from the evil one:

> Put on the whole armour of God, that ye may be able to stand against the wiles of the devil. For we wrestle not against flesh and blood but against principalities, against powers, against the rulers of the darkness of this world, against spiritual wickedness in high places (Eph. 6:11–18).

Read the rest of that passage and put on your own warm and secure robe.

6. *Money arguments.* Someone has said marriages aren't broken over the lack of sex or the lack of communication, but the lack of money.

> A shortage is a natural breeder of tension. We all know how easily our marriages can sputter, fume, and sizzle over the lack—real or imagined—of enough money to do what we and/or our wives want. Long after our sexual lives have been harmonized, our major career choices have been agreed upon, and the size of our family has been determined, we can still be hassling over money, with no solution in sight.[8]

I really agree with what Dean Merrill says here, that money itself is not the root of all evil, but rather the *love* of money, and it shouldn't be causing the problems it does. He says we should look on money as one of our "resources (along with time, energy, air, water, etc.), part of the raw material with which we build our lives." Money is a gift, a good and perfect gift of God, given according to His other gifts of talents, opportunities and jobs.

Mr. Merrill says you must think in terms of *our* money. Many women are going to work after years of guilt as the spender of "his" money and then creating two separate cash flows.

When I had a regular outside job I put my check into the pot alongside my husband's. It was *our* money and we spent it on our things—house, car, food, etc. I kept a small amount for spending and so did he. Now that I'm a keeper, my earnings aren't necessarily financial (in chapter 11 I tell how I save money by not working). My husband believes that what I do in maintaining our home and raising our children is as important as his job. He is happy to work hard in order to help make it happen. He doesn't begrudgingly hand over my weekly household finances—that is what he earned it for.

On the other hand, I am grateful to have financing for my projects, so I don't often spend more than he gives me, via charge accounts. Now that I earn a little money speaking and on book royalties I am able to buy him gifts that he doesn't have to pay for, a few things we both want for our house, and some clothes.

Some of the worst arguments we ever had were over money. This usually involved two areas: (1) we were suffering a setback or shortage and we each wanted to blame the other; (2) we became greedy over different business ventures that promised to make us rich.

When we just worked hard to get ourselves solvent again, we learned a lesson about overspending your budget and agreed to not let it happen again. I cut back on my areas of food, clothing, and home decorating. Marvin cut back on his big-car dream (he now drives a VW), which, at today's prices for cars and gas, is quite a saving.

My husband is basically a salesman and there are millions of opportunities to make it big in that field. Some time ago we both came to the realization that for us to "get rich quick" we would have to be totally committed to that goal. That interfered with our commitment to Jesus Christ, and it also interfered with our commitment to the quality of family life that we want to hand down to our children as a legacy far more valuable than money. Luke 3:14b says, "and be content with your wages." Hebrews 13:5, tells us "Let your conversation be without covetousness; and be content with such things as ye have. . . ." Philippians 4:11 puts it, "Not that I speak in respect of want: for I have learned, in whatsoever state I am, therewith to be content."

Contentment has to be one of the most wonderful blessings to be had. I don't mean that we should stop trying to better ourselves or that we should sit on a trash heap in rags and preach against "worldly things." I mean that once you are aware that *this is it,* job-wise, house-wise, car-wise, and all the rest, you give up the striving struggle, thank God for what you have, and *enjoy life.* Too many people strive too hard to achieve something that brings too little contentment when achieved.

Well, I hadn't intended to write a mini-marriage manual, but I believe it fills an essential part in the purpose of this chapter: to show how being a keeper at home benefits a marriage.

This chapter also brings us to a consideration of goals. If for your life-goal you have chosen being a wife and homemaker, then keep that preeminent. Make the "minor" goals you allow into your life those that will in the long run support your life-goal. For instance, if your family suffers a financial setback due to illness, it may be necessary for you to earn some money to help get you back on track. But be careful not to let the earning of money be your primary goal (which is easy to do once you begin earning). And before joining the many women who, like Kate, chose one goal but are ready to switch goals mid-stream, consider whether that's fair to the people involved in the first choice.

I hope there are no north winds blowing on your marriage. But, if there are, I hope you will be brave enough to drag out the quilts!

7. You Can Call Me Miss, Or You Can Call Me Mrs., But Don't Call Me Ms.!

> *For man does not originate from woman, but woman from man; for indeed man was not created for woman's sake, but woman for the man's sake.*
>
> 1 Corinthians 11:8,9

A recent New York AP clipping said, "American women say you can call them Mrs., or you can call them Miss, but you don't have to call them Ms."

During the National Organization for Women Conference in 1969, "Ms." was introduced as a designation intended as a feminist counterpart of "Mr.," a courtesy title that does not reveal a person's marital status.

A Virginia Slims American Women's Opinion Poll released the following information: "Only 16 percent of American women favor the title 'Ms.,' while 77 percent preferred 'Miss' or 'Mrs.'"

The *Lynchburg Daily Advance* reported that Betty Friedan, NOW founder, when asked for comment on the poll, said, "Perhaps you have to be mature to be called 'Ms.'"

Am I immature because I enjoy being "Mrs."? In Ms. Friedan's book *The Feminine Mystique*, she says women like me are suffering from being lulled into giving up the search for individual identity; that my person is submerged in my home, husband, and children.

O.K., Betty, so I'm immature because that *is* what I have done for the past fifteen years. What's going to happen to me now? She predicted that women like me would arrive at our middle years with a feeling of emptiness and would wind up on the psychiatrist's couch.

Well, I'm here (middle age), but I'm not there (psychiatrist's couch), and I still have my family. (The success of *The Feminine Mystique* swooped Friedan to the top of a burgeoning women's movement in the 1960s. She separated from her husband and moved from the suburbs to the city.)

In her fine book, *Let Me be a Woman*, Elisabeth Elliot says:

> The woman who defines her liberation as doing what she wants, or not doing what she doesn't want, is, in the first place, evading responsibility. Evasion of responsibility is the mark of immaturity. The Women's Liberation Movement is characterized, it appears, by this very immaturity. While telling themselves that they've come a long way, that they are actually coming of age, they have retreated to a partial humanity, one which refuses to acknowledge the vast significance of the sexual differentiation. (I do not say that they always ignore sexual differentiation itself, but that the *significance* of it escapes them entirely.) And the woman who ignores that fundamental truth ironically misses the very thing she has set out to find. By refusing to fulfill the whole vocation of womanhood, she settles for a caricature, a pseudopersonhood.[1]

I *have been* submerged in my family for years, but as they have less need of me, I see myself emerging from that protective cocoon in a full-fledged identity of my own. But, I didn't need to throw off the family to emerge and, like many women my age, I feel a new, exciting time is opening for me. I am contented, fulfilled, and happy. I am definitely not bored.

Judging by the many books I've read, Betty Friedan certainly has an identity of *her* own.

According to the 1977 *Good Housekeeping Woman's Almanac,*
Betty isn't bored either. She says: "I'm very unbored, I'm nasty, I'm
bitchy, I get mad. But, by God, I'm absorbed in what I'm doing."[2]
Now, I ask, is that mature? Or even happy?

It is just eighteen years since she accused advertisers, sociologists,
educators, and psychologists of selling the American woman the
myth of the "feminine mystique," that she could find total fulfillment through childbearing and homemaking, causing her to lose
her sense of identity because she had abandoned her own goals to
live through her family. And now I have the nerve to tell the
Christian woman to return home and submerge herself for a time in
the lives of her family?

Were we being sold a hyped "mystique" in the '50s? Or is it true,
women *do* find fullfillment in giving their lives for their families?
I'm not as bothered by the "feminine mystique" as I am the neglect
of the total female factor in our philosophy of life.

I *do* think full-time mothers begin their forties wondering who
they are and what they are going to do with the rest of their lives. I
wasn't always Mrs. Marvin Horton. I had an identity even in con-
ception. "My substance was not hid from thee, when I was made in
secret . . ." (Ps. 139:15a). I had an identity the moment I was
born. I was born female by God's design, and while I have been a
daughter, sister, wife, mother, daughter-in-law and mother-in-law,
I have never ceased being me. If being unrecognized is equated with
no identity, then most of the world has none.

I think the feminists have been selling us a hype job. Because
they are aggressive and vocal, they have almost even convinced
Christian women that they must be either unhappy or immature if
they aren't finding fulfillment outside the home.

Are Americans falling for the hype? Is marriage on the decline?
According to most studies, marriage is more popular than ever.

In November 1980, the *Lynchburg Advance* carried the following
article:

> Three-quarters of college students questioned in an unscientific sur-
> vey say they expect to be happily married and sexually faithful, though
> many say they expect the divorce rate to continue to climb.

"You have what I feel is a tremendous romantic naivete on the part of these undergraduates. They know what's going to happen, but they think it's not going to happen to them," Goldstein said.[3]

Why don't we work towards helping the dreams of these young people come true rather than dismissing them as illogical "romantics"? I think with a little bit of encouragement the pendulum can swing back to where, rather than living together or jumping in and out of marriage whenever the mood hits, couples will work at and fight for their marriages. Most divorces are granted because of incompatibility (except states where no-fault divorce exists). Almost all research indicates that opposites attract. We are *all* incompatible to start with. That's why making marriage work is so interesting.

I began this book with what I believed God was teaching me in Titus 2:1–5 about being a "keeper at home." Because I am now considered one of the aged women in that passage by my sheer survival as a Christian for fifteen years, it falls my privilege to share with many of the younger women who have asked me to teach them how to "love their own husbands" (Tit. 2:4) and to be "obedient" to them.

The first thing needed, I believe, is to fall in love with being married. Far from being passé, all signs indicate that Americans continue to believe fervently in marriage. A recent Gallup Poll shows that three out of four women in America say marriage and children are among the most important elements for fulfillment. "44 percent of the women would prefer not to have a job outside the home—they want to be full-time wives and mothers."[4]

You need to love the idea of marriage before you say yes to the man you love, because regardless of the removal by some women of *love, honor and obey* from their wedding vows, the Bible says that a woman is to be obedient to her own husband.

If that word strikes a raw nerve within you, you aren't alone. If I am to be honest, I must tell you that I have a stubborn streak of rebellion that waves a red flag at the word *obey*. Why should I obey anyone? Another word that made me breathe fast was *submit*.

The first time I heard a message on wives being submissive, taken from Ephesians 5:22–23, I balked, rebelled, squawked, and hated the very idea.

You wives must submit to your husbands' leadership in the same way you submit to the Lord. For a husband is in charge of his wife in the same way Christ is in charge of his body the Church. (He gave His very life to take care of it and be its Saviour!) So you wives must willingly obey your husbands in everything, just as the Church obeys Christ" (TLB).

"That's out of the Dark Ages!" I cried. I felt my new-found peace slipping out through my pores the more I rejected this principle laid down by God.

I began to understand the precious truth of this principle one Sunday morning, seated in a church I had consented to go to only because it had an outstanding youth program. The reason I was there *only* because of the youth program was that I strongly disliked the ways of the pastor. He seemed not only dogmatic but bulldog-matic on many issues, especially that of wives being in submission. I still believe he might have found a more loving, humorous way of presenting the topic without making women feel inferior. (There's that streak again!)

Regardless of my thoughts on the subject, it seemed that God had called him, not me, to pastor the church.

That Sunday I had planned to use sermon time to study for my own Bible classes. However, I couldn't collect my thoughts through his red-faced yelling against sin and the constant "whop" of a Bible on the pulpit.

What I recognized to be the "still, small voice" of the Lord I loved, but was failing to obey, started messing with the ear of my heart. He tapped me on the shoulder and said, "You aren't enjoying the service much, are you?"

"No, I never do." I began realizing at once an attitude problem and was reminded of a verse in Romans 13:1. I quickly turned there to read: "Let every soul be subject unto the higher powers. For there is no power but of God: The powers that be are ordained of God." God seemed to be saying, "I didn't bring *you* to this church because of the youth ministry. I brought your children here for that. But I have a lesson especially prepared for your life. That man preaching is ordained by me to preach and you are to be subject to him."

I stared at the short man jumping up and down behind the pulpit and asked, "Me? Be in submission to *him?*"

"That's right, because in submitting to him, you are actually submitting to My power. Does that make it any easier?"

Squirming uneasily in the padded pew, not hearing anything but the Voice of God speaking through His written Word, "Submit, surrender, submit, *submit,*" I cried out silently in grief over my stubborn heart. "O God, I'm sorry. I can't submit now, but I'm willing to be made willing to submit. Help my unbelief!"

That prayer was the first step that changed my entire life—my church life, my married life, and even my civil life. God opened up my eyes to an important truth: our placement on His organizational chart has nothing to do with our individual worth.

Beverly LaHaye says that submission is an attitude of obedience.

> The woman who is truly spirit-filled will want to be totally submissive to her husband. Regardless of what the current trend towards Women's Lib advocates, anything which departs from God's design for women is not right. Submission does not mean that she is owned and operated by her husband but that he is the head or manager. A manager knows how to develop and use the gifts in others. This is what God intended the husband to do for the wife. He helps her develop to her greatest potential. He keeps track of the overall picture but puts her in charge of areas where she functions well. This is a truly liberated woman. Submission is God's design for woman. Christ's example teaches that true submission is neither reluctant nor grudging, nor is it a result of imposed authority; it is rather an act of worship to God when it is a chosen, deliberate, voluntary response to a husband.[5]

I began to remember different government offices in which I had worked. They each had organizational charts and, while there were people of different ranking on those charts, each job was important to the whole organization. My boss, the director of research, could spend his entire life conducting research, but if someone failed to type it and collate it, it would have been of little value.

In God's organizational chart according to Galatians 3:28 (RSV), "there is neither Jew nor Greek, there is neither slave nor free, there is neither male nor female; for you are all one in Christ Jesus."

There it is—in God's eyes we are completely equal. He knows that what we need for living on earth is *organization* and He selected the male factor to be in command in the family, with the female next in the chain.

In her book *Love, Honor and Be Free,* Maxine Hancock says,

> Now this opens up a prospect to me which is far more inviting than that of being "put in my place." Given to me is the opportunity of accepting a position—not as a sign of subservience or an acquiescence to inferior status—but as a voluntary, rational acceptance that God has made an order which is for the good of men and women alike and which, followed, will produce the greatest human happiness.[6]

Mrs. Hancock says that the woman following this approach to submission finds herself being "conformed to the image of his Son" (Rom. 8:29).

Last spring I picked strawberries in two locations. One was what I considered the best deal—free strawberries! The friend who offered them to me told me to come on over but just be careful and not step on the berries. No problem, I thought. There *was* a problem because the plants were everbearing and had multiplied and the whole garden was overrun with plants and berries. I picked in every position; I stepped on berries, kneeled on berries, and managed to pick a few quarts before my back went out completely.

Some days later I went to a strawberry farm. What a difference. The plants were in neat rows and I could sit or kneel in one spot and pick quarts of the luscious berries. I probably got thirty quarts in the same length of time I got three in the other garden. Why the difference? Organization.

Major responsibilities and decision-making have to be assumed by someone in order to prevent disorder in business. In sports, the coach makes decisions about a certain play and the player makes the move. The whole team wins or loses the game.

NOW stands for National Organization for Women. The middle word is *organization* and I'm sure there are many submissive, hardworking people in it. I wonder how Betty Friedan, its leader, would feel if all her secretaries protested their boring, mundane, dead-end jobs and decided they wanted to be boss. What if the janitor struck for a desk job? That would be foolish—Ms. Friedan is boss because she founded the organization and somebody has to clean the bathrooms, so the janitor had better do the job or be replaced.

Well, God founded marriage—He is Boss and He has selected the male factor to be next in command. That's just the way it is.

When I began to see that as organizational charts worked in business and in sports they must work in church and home too, my attitude began changing.

About this time I also had the privilege of attending a Basic Youth Conflicts Seminar conducted by Bill Gothard. I will forever be grateful for his loving, tender placing of each family member in his Chain of Command principle, because it makes us all accountable to someone—my husband to God—me to my husband—and the children to us. It makes sense, but even if it didn't, it works!

> The Positive Woman recognizes that there is a valid and enduring purpose behind this recognition of different roles for men and women which is just as relevant in the twentieth century as it was in the time of Saint Paul. . . .
> Any successful vehicle must have one person at the wheel with ultimate responsibility. . . . A family cannot be run by committee. The committee system neutralizes a family with continuing controversy and encumbers it with psychological impediments. It makes a family as clumsy and slow as a hippopotamus (which might be defined as a racehorse designed by committee).[7]

A few weeks after my close encounter with a displeased Lord, with my Bible opened to the text of the day, I looked up at the same pulpit and saw a different man. He was still short, but I saw that his fiery delivery and pulpit-banging were from anger over the sin that is wrecking our homes and stealing our children. I saw he had put his life into protecting our basic family structure. I saw that, in love, he knew I would be safer under the protective tent of my own husband, ideally. Why was I now seeing what I had failed to see before? Could it be that the chip I was carrying on my shoulder interefered with my vision?

The tent under which I take shelter has a name printed across the top—PROTECTION. There are many stakes securing this tent, but there are three main ones.

Stake 1: Physical Protection. This stake holds up the part of the tent protecting me from physical, male labor such as chopping down trees or fighting on the front lines. Although, in our law, a woman who chooses to lay cross-ties or drive earth-moving equipment has to be given equal opportunity and pay,[8] I don't choose to do that, and my husband would die for my right to be a woman. He further protects me from *physical attack* and makes sure our home is secure. Call me old-fashioned, but I feel good about the sock in the nose he would give some man who made ugly advances toward me or my daughter. He has already protected me physically by providing the proper care when I was seriously ill for several years with multiple sclerosis.

Whenever I counsel a woman who is breaking up her marriage for an affair, I have to ask her: If, after your husband, who may still love you, moves out and starts his life over again—if you should come down with M.S. as I did, who would care for you? Could you expect a lover who was attracted to you first by your looks to care for you, especially if you couldn't reward his sexual advances? Would he stick by you when you, made ugly by disease, had little hope for normality? Part of the physical protection provided under the tent called "My Husband" is sacrificed in the blindness some call "love," most of which is infatuation. That fire will die out.

Stake 2: Emotional Protection. Because I gave myself unconditionally and completely to my husband, he assumed the care of my emotional well-being. The very nature of being female includes some emotional upheaval through hormonal changes the male doesn't have. Because God tells him to love me as Christ loves the church, he has learned over the years to be sensitive to areas in which I am weak. As our boys were growing up, there were sometimes problems with other children, teachers, or neighbors. My husband's emotional support was all-important.

He has also protected me from our own children by admonishing, "you are to obey your mother, and if you sass her you will have to deal with me. And if you ever think, *even think,* of laying one hand on her, you'd better be packed." I was never physically threatened by them, but there were a lot of "deal-with-me" times. Our children not only have active bodies and minds but mouths that sometimes open before their minds are in gear.

One of the neatest things about this part of the tent is that when I am emotionally drained and feel like giving up, these strong arms come out and hold me and somehow, I know as long as we have each other, it will be O.K. This is usually a temporary retreat on my part, a time for emotional rest. It does not mean I have, as Betty Friedan says, a "weak ego or sense of self"; I am not "renouncing active aims, ambitions or interest in one's own life to live through others."

In his book *Burn-Out*, Dr. H. J. Freudenberger points out that no matter what career choices we make for our lives, burn-out is a real threat. It is a growing weary of doing the same thing over and over. It is a growing cynicism and hardness that leads to fatigue, sleep disturbances, inability to cope with tasks that were always easy, depression. In its severest forms, burn-out can lead to a desire to run away or to commit suicide. Whether we are social workers who have seen too much suffering and insensitivity or housewives who have seen too many washers full of clothes, we are all susceptible to burn-out. We may need a change of direction or priorities, to take a closer look at what we are becoming. We may even search the Bible for spiritual solutions but come up empty because we are dealing with an emotional response to a life situation. Emotional disturbances of anger and bitterness may lead to spiritual holocaust.

In dealing with these problems, we need a human being who cares about us. That's why building and maintaining the right marriage relationship is so vital. Part of the time I need the emotional vacation and part of the time my husband does. When I'm up, perhaps he is down and vice versa.

In an interview on the subject of burn-out, I heard a woman tell of burning out at home, poring over the want ads, and dreaming of a better life. She responded to one of the ads, took a job that soon became boring, and burned out there too. Her question was: "Where do I go now?"

Another woman said, "I *do* think of me first. I pamper myself. If I don't want to cook, I don't. If I want to go away for three days, I just go. But I am suffering the same symptoms of burn-out." The doctor jokingly replied, "You are suffering from recreation burn-out."

It isn't an exterior problem but an interior one, pointed out another woman who grabbed the mike on the Donahue show. "Who is happier—my mom who did all the 'supermom,' at-home things and never complained? Who knows, maybe she was just a silent sufferer. But I am the super-achiever with the great career with good money and I suffer too. Who is the winner anyway?"

Stake 3: Spiritual Protection. Adam was given spiritual authority when God commanded him not to eat of the tree of good and evil, lest he die (spiritual death, not physical). When Adam passed this tidbit on to Eve that made her subordinate by process of elimination. Common sense tells me that if my husband were to say, "Marilee, God has given me a command," I would discuss it first with him before taking advice from a third party that would negate his wishes.

That does not make Eve inferior nor does it make me inferior. Eleanor Roosevelt said, "No one can make you feel inferior without your consent."

Maxine Hancock asks in *Love, Honor and be Free*, "Did Satan come to her because she was the 'weaker sex'?" She believes Eve was vulnerable to subtle temptation, "just because she was in a position of subordination to her husband."

> Satan's temptation to her was to make a spiritual decision on her own, against the command of God expressed to her by her husband. Satan urged her to repeat his sin: that of rebellion against divine authority, the usurpation of authority by a subordinate. Thus, as Satan had said in his heart, "I will ascend into heaven, I will exalt my throne above the stars of God . . . I will be like the most high" (Isa. 13–14), so he invited Eve to rebel against the authority of her husband in order that together they could "be as gods" (Gen. 3:5).[9]

Mrs. Hancock concludes that it was Eve's disobedience to Adam that actually led to disobedience to God and introduced the human race to sin.

Well, Eve, you blew it! It seemed like such a small thing, taking a piece of fruit. I have committed acts of disobedience that seemed much worse than that, so I can't be too hard on you. But then why are so many of your sisters complaining about their lot? You can't disobey without paying the consequences of that disobedience.

When Eve refused to voluntarily accept the role of subordination, she was forced to experience subjection. Again, I emphasize, subordination is not bad; the second and third persons of the Trinity are subordinate to the first person. Would anyone like to say that God the Son is inferior to God the Father?

When I take spiritual leadership from my husband, I leave myself open for attack, much as Eve did. My husband travels a great deal, and that places me as spiritual leader at home when he is away. That's different. If your husband refuses spiritual leadership for your family, then you must do the best you can with it without shaming him or making him feel inferior. But if we take over spiritual leadership responsibilities because we think we have an "in" with God, beware! It can hinder our mate's growth, set a precedent for our children's home and place on us heavy burdens we will burn out bearing.

I'm not advocating our being doormats. If God meant for men to marry doormats, it would have been easier for Him to come up with a robot than the complicated complement He created. You are a *person*. If you deny your personhood, you may become a thing or a slave. Now, any man would probably like a slave to order around— for awhile. But he really wants someone to share his life with.

You also have a mind as good as his, and I believe you should, early in marriage, expect at least to be heard. If our minds are good and we never express what is in them, we may be cheating the partnership. We can speak with a soft voice, a humble spirit, and a willingness to prefer his way over our own, if push comes to shove.

A beautiful picture of true submission was painted for me a few years ago.

One September afternoon, in the tropical heat of Tampa, I was being interviewed by a reporter, Jane Jones, (not her real name) who was strongly committed to the feminist movement. I shared my testimony and she shared her views. The conversation became heated too as she told of her trip to the NOW conference in Texas, though it was only when questioned that she mentioned the ugly demonstrations, the foul language and "railroad" tactics.

After the interview, I invited this widowed, attractive mother of four to be my guest at a Christian women's retreat. "Why not come and observe 600 Christian women in action and report (if you dare) on the difference between your brand of 'liberation' and ours, through Christ?" She agreed and we drove to Orlando a few weeks later in a state of perpetual conversation.

"Marilee, can't you see that men want to dominate women and keep them subservient? They know once we taste freedom and equality, we will never be content in the home again."

"But, Jane, I don't want to be 'not content' in the home, number 1. And number 2, my marriage isn't like that. My husband is good to always allow me to attend things like this and he trusts me to do what I feel I should do. I can go to work tomorrow if I want to."

RED FLAG! She became livid as I obviously hit a button.

"What do you mean, *allows* you to go? Does he ask your permission before he does anything? I just bet he doesn't!"

That discussion lasted until the next morning when it was time to get ready for the meetings. Since she had also told me that she thought Buddha was as much God as Jesus was, I assumed that she was not a believer. I felt I just couldn't run off with my friends (although I was sure I was missing lots of fun while I stayed with her to argue).

I was putting on my pantyhose while Jane was in the bathroom applying makeup.

"Jane, there's a prayer meeting in Kay's room at nine. Would you like to go?"

"Whatever you want to do is fine with me."

Sensing she might be uneasy, I said, "Really, now, I don't mind missing if you feel you would be uncomfortable."

Her reply was good-natured. "Hey, that's okay. If I don't have to pray out loud, I don't mind going."

"Are you sure?"

"Come on, let's go."

I burst out laughing, "Hey, Jane, do you know what we just did?"

"No, what?" She was puzzled.

"You are in submission to me! You just gave in to my wishes, but I was willing to submit to yours. We did it out of respect for each other and we did it in a kind way, but someone was bound to win. This time I won, but next time you may. In fact, I owe you one.

That's it! Jane, that's it! That's what I've been trying to tell you Ephesians 5:21 says: 'Submitting yourselves one to another in the fear of God.' You see, it isn't order-barking submission but a kind, humble bowing to the desires of another because you care about each other. It *is* an attitude!"

She thought silently for a moment. "That makes more sense than anything I've heard on the subject. Let's get to that prayer meeting."

Later we discussed all sorts of living arrangements from the typical marriage to homosexual relationships and agreed that where two people meet and are attracted to each other, one in all probability will have stronger leadership qualities than the other. The other person will probably submit more to that person, and not mind at all.

The happy ending to that story is that Jane accepted Christ as her Savior that weekend. She also went home and wrote a beautiful article for the Sunday paper about the peaceful way the 600 glowing women got along with each other. She spoke of the peace they exhibited and attributed that to their having found purpose for their lives.

Submission is only *one* of the keys to a happy marriage.

Actress Glynis Johns said, "I refuse to be unhappy—unhappiness is a habit."

And Helen Keller said, "Joy is the holy fire that keeps our purpose warm and our intelligence aglow."

Two social scientists, Paul Ammons, assistant professor of social work and child and family development at the University of Georgia, and Nick Stinnett, professor and chairman of the Department of Human Development and the Family College of Home Economics at the University of Nebraska, determined to find marriages that could be considered joyful. They were frustrated by their realization that most research is focused on unhappy families.

For the project, families that had been together ten or more years, with at least one child, and who appeared to have a strong relationship, were selected.

The report of their study based on marriage-quality questionnaires, was the subject of an article by Sally Wendkos Olds, *"Do*

You Have What it Takes to Make a Good Marriage?" that appeared in the October 1980 issue of *Ladies Home Journal.* While current statistics show that one of every two marriages end in divorce, and in spite of headlines telling us that marriage is "outdated," "irrelevant," "incompatible with personal fulfillment," strong, happy marriages *do* exist, and the study helped reveal the mysterious people involved in vital marriages.

The term "vital marriage" was coined by sociologists J. F. Cuber and P. B. Harroff. It refers to the "ideal relationship most of us yearn for—one in which two people find their prime joy in life in each other, yet still maintain separate identities."

The question that needed answering was: "What makes some of us capable of forming attachments that bring fulfillment and delight to our lives?"

The results were exciting. The study of over 400 families seemed to substantiate the thought that true happiness and fulfillment comes only as we unfold and develop our lives according to the purpose God has for *each individual.* According to the research, the key to success seems to lie "not so much in what these couples *do* but in the kind of people they *are."*

Ammons and Stinnett, while acknowledging that all good marriages are not alike nor is there an "ideal" personality in every couple, they did find certain characteristics that turned up much more often among the "vital" couples than among the less contented couples. It was on this basis that the researchers compiled a profile of the happily married person.

I couldn't help making some comparisons between what these secular researchers found and what the Bible has to say.

1. *"People in vital marriages are giving people."* The report indicated that in an age that urges you to "do whatever makes you feel good" or to "do your own thing," these people were meeting their own emotional needs by doing for others. They "yearn to be nurturers, to offer help, sympathy, kindness—and they do it not out of charity but for their own fulfillment." The article spoke of psychologist Gerhard Neubeck, former president of the National Council on Family Relations, who had described his feelings: "When I bring my wife a cup of coffee in the morning I know that it gives her

pleasure, but I enjoy it too. Her face lights up. She says, 'Thank you,' and our day is off to a good start."[10]

The people questioned did not think of themselves as martyrs nor do they keep score. Their need to be caring seemed to be every bit as important as their spouse's need to be cared for.

Scripture gives the basis for what these couples have discovered:

> Love endures long and is patient and kind; love never is envious nor boils over with jealousy; is not boastful or vainglorious, does not display itself haughtily. It is not conceited—arrogant and inflated with pride; it is not rude (unmannerly), and does not act unbecomingly. Love [God's love in us] does not insist on its own rights or its own way, for it is not self-seeking; it is not touchy or fretful or resentful; it takes no account of the evil done to it—pays no attention to a suffered wrong (1 Cor. 13:1, 4–5 AB).

Whether or not the respondents to the questionnaire are Christians is not relevant to my obedience. I am a Christian and I am to obey a higher law—God who asks me to be enduring, patient, kind, mannerly, not self-seeking. I also know that God never asks me to do something that He won't give me the power to do.

2. *"They have a strong sense of commitment to their marriages."* Donna Anderson from Minneapolis said she and her husband "have built something over the past nineteen years and we want to hang onto it. We don't believe in a throwaway society."[10] Others spoke of marriage as a living thing and the need to fight as hard for marriage as for your own life.

> But from the beginning of creation God made them male and female. For this reason a man shall leave (behind) his father and mother and be joined to his wife, and cleave closely to her (permanently). And two shall become one flesh, so that they are no longer two, but one flesh. What therefore God has united—joined together—let not man separate or divide (Mark 10:6–9, AB).

Individual Christians and churches are rightfully meeting the ever-increasing needs of divorced brothers and sisters. But I wonder if we aren't adapting our churches more to meet a humanistic approach (forming more classes for divorced people) than helping couples work *one step at a time* towards building what God has called them to—a lifelong, moment-by-moment, day-by-day, growing marriage relationship.

3. *"They are strong-minded."* It seemed that while marital harmony was top priority for most of these couples who were interviewed, as individuals they valued their own opinions and did not feel inferior.

> Fill up and complete my joy by living in harmony and being of the same mind and one in purpose . . . being in full accord and of one harmonious mind and intention. Do nothing from factional motives—through contentiousness, strife, selfishness or for unworthy ends—or prompted by conceit and empty arrogance. Instead, in the true spirit of humility (lowliness of mind) let each regard the others as better than and superior to himself—thinking more highly of one another than you do of yourselves (Phil. 2:2–4, AB).

This Scripture does not conflict with the strong, healthy self-images projected by these successful couples. It doesn't just say "wives, think of yourself lower than your husband," it says "let each. . . ." Again, this is an attitude of considering the other person first. If you both have the same strong ideas about marriage and family, you won't feel threatened by being exposed to new ideas in other areas.

4. *"They had vigorous sexual drives."* The respondents indicated a mutual admiration for the sexual blessings a marriage affords. The very idea of permanence takes away the element of "You can be replaced" and puts in its place a willingness to learn new ways of pleasing each other.

I find it difficult to understand how couples who play the multiple-mating game don't ever seem to realize that the depth and beauty they are seeking through sex-with-many can only be enjoyed by sexual growth that may take many years. I suppose every couple looks back on their first years of constant and instant glandular attraction with a smile. It may not be constant nor instant any more but I would agree with many of the couples responding—it is richer, more fulfilling, warmer and, yes, even better than it was when we were supposedly at our sexual peak.

The Bible has so much to say about sex that it is a mystery to me that the Victorian age got away with describing a woman who enjoyed sex as a "loose or immoral woman."

Maxine Hancock says in *Love, Honor and be Free:*

> This is not to suggest that the wife should accept a role of passivity—something which has long since been repudiated by women. (And really, I wonder just how many Victorian wives really found sex as uninteresting as this century's critics would like to suppose. I like a line in Jessamyn West's *The Friendly Persuasion:* "Eliza [Quaker wife and mother] looked at the face that had always pleasured her." I have a hunch that lots of husbands "pleasured" lots of wives long before sexual liberty was announced by the Kinsey report.)
>
> Voluntary submissiveness in sex is far from passivity; it is, rather, an active desire to please and give pleasure to the other partner.[11]

It is also hard to believe that today's Christian women look on sex as something to be endured as part of their whole "submissive role." The keeper at home has much to do with the keeper of good sex in the marriage. Where was she when I was young?

> Drink waters out of your own cistern [of pure marriage relationship], and fresh running waters out of your own well . . . [Confine yourself to your own wife]. . . . Let your fountain—of human life—be blessed [with the rewards of fidelity], and rejoice with the wife of your youth. Let her be as the loving hind and pleasant doe [tender, gentle, attractive]; let her bosom satisfy you at all times; and always be transported with delight in her love (Prov. 5:15–20, AB).

5. *"They like to talk."* The couples responding to the survey had learned to talk about everything and weren't afraid to be open and direct in expressing their feelings. Like all couples, they sometimes disagree but have developed the art of communication to the point of resolving conflicts quickly, forgiving quickly, and not carrying grudges.

Often the working wife keeps to herself the things happening to her at work or in her personal growth, either listening to her husband and children or blocking them out of her tired mind.

> Rather, let our lives lovingly express truth in all things. . . . When angry, do not sin; do not ever let your wrath—your exasperation, your fury or indignation—last until the sun goes down. . . . Let no foul or polluting language, nor evil word, nor unwholesome or worthless talk [ever] come out of your mouth; but only such [speech] as is good and beneficial to the spiritual progress of others, as is fitting to the need and the occasion, that it may be a blessing . . ." (Eph. 4:15, 26, 29, AB).

6. *"They have a positive outlook on life."* Most couples who have enjoyed long marriages look back on the crisis times as the most bonding, strengthening and beneficial times in the history of their relationship. Mind-feeding and control is the secret.

> . . . Whatever is true, whatever is worthy of reverence and is honorable and seemly, whatever is just, whatever is pure, whatever is lovely and lovable, whatever is kind and winsome and gracious, if there is any virtue and excellence, if there is anything worthy of praise, think on and weigh and take account of these things—fix your minds on them. (Phil. 4:8, AB).

7. *"They don't take good things for granted."* The couples questioned seemed quick to express praise and appreciation for each other. If we can ever get on the "grateful train" we go from car to car enjoying the contents whether they be a good day's health, a comfortable bed, a good cup of coffee, or even an aspirin, if you have a headache. When you take that train to other countries and see people without the basics it makes our debates seem so small.

> Thank [God] in everything—no matter what the circumstances may be, be thankful and give thanks; for this is the will of God for you [who are] in Christ Jesus . . . (1 Thess. 5:18, AB).

8. *"They are sensitive to other people."* Ammons and Stinnett said they were struck with the respect the couples showed for each other. They called this "otherness," as opposed to "self-ness." They

said that the sensitivity was the primary reason the couples could build and maintain strong relationships.

> Look not every man on his own things, but every man also on the things of others. (Phil. 2:4, AB).

9. *"They are deeply spiritual."* My heart skipped a beat as I read this. Of course they are! The reason so many other couples are failing in their marriages is that they failed to deal with the spiritual aspects of their whole being. We are created spiritual beings and marriage is a picture of a heavenly truth—Christ and His Bride, His church. Humanly speaking, there probably are not solutions to the marital messes we see. But we are not to be just humans; we are to be spiritual humans.

> For other foundation can no man lay than that is laid, which is Jesus Christ (1 Cor. 3:11).

Marriage is a uniquely spiritual affair and those who try to make it work apart from spiritual principles are swimming upstream all the way.

I have often felt out of step as I refused to march to the feminist drummer, but I see that there are many women in the same parade I'm in. We are practicing our steps and honing our talents because we have almost selfishly seen that we are the ones to gain in the long run. So, actually, we *are* doing our own thing.

Women like me, who have had strong feminist views early in their lives, seem to have different views as the years roll by. One such woman was Ruth Benedict. She began with traditional female roles as wife, teacher, and social worker. She had many choices open to her and she took advantage of them. By the time she was thirty-four years old she had given up on her marriage and put her Vassar education to use by becoming a leading anthropologist in the mid-1940s.

I had been misled by a statement taken out of context, printed in feminist literature, attributed to Mrs. Benedict: "To me it seems a very terrible thing to be a woman."

I mentally listed her on the feminists' side until I read the rest of her statement in Elisabeth Elliot's *Let Me be a Woman:*

> Ruth Benedict, one of the first women to attain recognition as a major social scientist, wrote in her journal in 1912: "To me it seems a very terrible thing to be a woman. There is one crown which perhaps is worth it all—a great love, a quiet home, and children. [Her childless marriage to Stanley Benedict ended in divorce.] We must all know that is all that is worthwhile, and we must peg away, showing off our wares on the market if we have money, or manufacturing careers for ourselves if we haven't. We have not the motive to prepare ourselves for a 'lifework' of teaching, of social work—we know we would lay it down with hallelujah in the height of our success, to make a home for the right man. And all the time in the background of our consciousness rings the warning that perhaps the right man will never come. A great love is given to very few. Perhaps this makeshift time-filler of a job *is* our lifework after all."[12]

Humanly speaking, the women's movement has a point. If life was fair and just, why should the woman be so responsible for so much? How can we make sense out of such hard work for so little earthly return? I think Colossians 3:17 is placed in a strategic location. Just prior to the instruction for husbands loving their wives, wives submitting, children obeying and fathers not provoking, comes this verse: "And whatsoever ye do in word or deed, do all in the name of the Lord Jesus, giving thanks to God and the Father by him" (Col. 3:17, KJV).

How can we live a life so at odds with the *Cosmopolitan* woman who is demanding and getting her rights? I think the key is these words found in Colossians 1:27: ". . . Christ *in you*, the hope of glory" (KJV).

Christ, who came to live His life through us, has always been at odds with the world system, so it stands to reason that if He *is* living in us, we will find it just as much so. While the liberated, modern world may point a finger at such backwoods ideas, God has promised special blessings and rewards for those lives.

Sometimes I feel hypocritical because part of me likes my independent ideas and opinions as well as the fulfillment I find in areas outside my marriage, and the other part enjoys a real old-fashioned marriage. Is something wrong with me that I can't choose between the two? Or, is it possible I have reached a scriptural yet personally satisfactory place that is occupied by multitudes of women who have not been heard from?

We haven't been heard from because we aren't angry enough to march and write books nor do we feel we have any magic ingredients (like wrapping in plastic wrap and lying on the dining room table). We have found a way that works and perhaps we don't quite know why, so we are reluctant to talk about it except on a one-to-one level.

Perhaps I just don't believe in the extremes of having to toss one thing over to have the other. I believe that God *did* create me equal and that He is not sexist. I find comfort in knowing that I am here for a specific purpose and that my life counts as much as any man's. While I tenaciously hang onto that precious individualism, seeking to find my purpose, I need not toss out my marriage. In fact, the marriage is the comforting incubator from which I emerge, stronger and more sufficient each day—that is, if I don't view my marriage as something holding me down.

Yes, marriage is restrictive. Spending the past twenty-five years with one husband has set certain limitations on my lifestyle. But that is not a negative thing for me, because I came into my marriage as an insecure young woman and the restrictions provided me with a plan, some order, and lots of security.

Marriage is old-fashioned. Old in everything from art and coins to automobiles is considered synonymous with antiquity and preciousness. So why is old-fashioned marriage synonymous with bad? It didn't take much intelligence on the part of a person in our neighborhood to discard an old lamp. But, once we retrieved it, cleaned it up, and it was appraised as an antique crystal lamp of value, we found it worthy of preserving and keeping. It all boils down to how much each of us valued that lamp. The same can be true of marriage—it takes no great intelligence to see the absurdity of throwing matrimony out of the door in the name of freedom.

A contented emotional response is not determined by whether or not the homemaker leaves the home to develop a career. If this were the case, there would not be so many discontented, gainfully employed mothers feeling guilt and frustration. On the other hand, there are numerous women at home who never leave "to seek their fortune," yet they are equally frustrated and upset.

It is not the career; it is not the home; it is the attitude of the heart and the response to God's command [that] . . . produces a better self-image . . . develops a warmer relationship between a woman and her husband, enables her to establish a home atmosphere of love and learning for the children, and even allows her to accomplish outside achievements that reach beyond her greatest expectations.[13]

To which drummer are you marching?

8. I Thought It Came Naturally

> A family is an ecologically balanced environment for
> the growth of human beings.
>
> Edith Schaeffer

Somewhere between 6:15 and 6:20 P.M. on a crackly cold January 13, 1981, a cataclysmic event that even agnostics call miraculous, occurred in a hall outside a delivery room. Mark (our second son), holding Laura's perspiring hand, instructed her to puff while he rang for a nurse. Without the presence of a physician (who had gone home for dinner), the nurse instructed Mark to don a gown and assist in the birth of the baby boy we had all been anxiously awaiting.

The immense joy, of a new flavor, could only be expressed in tears mingling with the sweat as a healthy, eight-pound Ryan Elliott Horton was first placed on Laura's exhausted abdomen and then into the proud daddy's shaking hands. Many hospitals are now allowing the parents those first sensitive minutes to begin a natural process now thought to be vital to a child's later development. It is called "bonding," and for Mark and Laura it was love at first sight.

I join the ranks of writers who try, ever so feebly, to express the emotions felt at this time. While extra time was allowed for beginning the love affair by skin contact with the baby (it must be something like animals who lick their newborns to stimulate), no one had to teach them to love him—not there, not in Lamaze class, nor in the multitude of books they had read.

While we aren't clear about the precise moment the baby pushed his way into the world, due to the unusual circumstances surrounding the birth, we are sure of one thing: Between 6:15 and 6:20 P.M. that same date, at least three children were being attacked by a parent who perhaps had experienced the same joy and love that Mark and Laura had at their son's birth. Why? Because every two minutes in our country a child is attacked and abused by its parents. What happens that gives Dr. Vincent J. Fontana, Medical Director of New York City's Foundling Hospital, cause to say:

> Parents bash, lash, beat, flay, stomp, suffocate, strangle, gut-punch, choke with rags or hot pepper, poison, crack heads open, slice, rip, steam, fry, boil, dismember. They use fists, belt buckles, straps, hairbrushes, lamp cords, sticks, baseball bats, rulers, shoes, boots, lead or iron pipes, bottles, brick walls, bicycle chains, pokers, knives, scissors, chemicals, lighted cigarettes, boiling water, steaming radiators, and open gas flames.[1]

I cringe as I type those graphic words. They make my skin crawl, my stomach ache, and my eyes fill up. I also cringe because I know they will rudely crash into your day and cause those same reactions. But I type them because Dr. Fontana declares that it is a myth that in this nation we love our children. Child abuse, he says, is the number one killer of American children, ". . . probably the most common cause of death in children today, outnumbering those caused by any of the infectious diseases, leukemia or automobile accidents." The American Humane Association reported the abuse of 307,000 children in 1975 alone. How many hundreds of thousands went unreported that year? This year? The annual report of sexual abuse is put at from fifty to seventy-five thousand. New York City alone has thirty thousand reported abuse cases a year. One hundred thousand children in this country are emotionally neglected and another one hundred thousand are physically, morally, and educationally neglected. . . . At least seven hundred are killed by their parents or parent surrogates.[2]

As a result of abuse of neglect, children run away from home at the rate of one million a year. Thirty children per day commit suicide in this country, according to a recent television news commentary.

Dale Evans says in *Hear the Children Crying*, "If the rate continues to rise as it is rising now, we can expect to find ourselves faced with a figure of a million and a half children either seriously maimed or crippled or killed annually."[3]

Is lack of love the cause for beating children? Not usually. Read this heartbreaking letter from an abusive mother:

> Although I love him very much, my nervousness leads me to do things I often disapprove of at the time, and if I don't disapprove of my actions at this time, I frequently disapprove of them later . . . many times. After I beat him he would lie in his crib and cry himself to sleep. I would sit next to the crib and cry and wish I could beat myself.[4]

For an examination of love that comes naturally and love that must be taught, let's look at parental love on four levels.

Level 1 Love: Affectionate Parenting

The kind of love Mark and Laura experienced as they held their slippery, pink newborn was probably identical with the feelings of the abusive mother above as she held her newborn. It is actually instinctive love, innate under normal circumstance, but according to Dr. John Kennell, not always instantaneous.

> Yet even "early contact" doesn't guarantee love at first sight. . . . About 40 percent of mothers fall in love when their babies are still in the womb. For about 25 percent it happens shortly after birth. But other mothers wait as much as a week, a month, or more before bonding takes place.[5]

It is an almost romantic, idealistic love that begins, often while the mother is making the nursery ready, and it feels quite special, almost mysterious. Beverly LaHaye says: "The woman has the unique opportunity to develop a close, working relationship with God, as He creates life within her."[6]

This level of love has much to do with images and perceptions of what you and your baby will be. It includes that overwhelming feeling the first time you hold your baby to your breast or look at him while he sleeps. Level 1 love contains the mother's ambitions to be a good mother and her dreams for the child, and while he remains a sleeping baby, the dream lives on. During the image-making stage, most mothers-to-be expect to be the perfect mother, not making the mistakes they observe others making.

While affectionate parenting seems to come naturally during this stage, it is not to be taken lightly.

> Theodore Lidz, Chairman of the Department of Psychiatry at Yale University School of Medicine, states emphatically that "during no other period of life is the person so transformed both physically and developmentally as during infancy." He further affirms that "no part of his life experience will be as solidly incorporated in the individual, become so irrevocably a part of him, as his infancy." Lack of physical care can result in ill health, wasting away, and death. Lack of social nurturing will result in distortions of emotional development and stunting of intellectual growth.
>
> Even an improper diet can influence the infant's lifetime intellectual capacity, since all of the nerve and brain cells a person will ever have are produced by six months of age.[7]

Who is at fault for the many mentally and emotionally deficient children coming out of the ghetto and the low-income housing projects? Are the older women so anxious to get into the work force that they don't have time to teach the younger women how very important it is for their infant's entire future to have bonding and nurturing? Has anyone ever told them how vital protein is to the building brain cells and that putting Kool-Aid or cola drinks in their bottles is damaging?

A few years ago I visited a children's TB hospital in Haiti where many malnourished babies and children were finally being properly nourished in a clean and comfortable setting. While the disease had progressed to different stages in the children, there were some with bloated stomachs, marked by surgery scars, who seemed lively and ran up for my husband and me to hold them. Others who weren't nearly as ill just lay on their bare cots in lethargy and sadness.

Upon inquiry the doctor explained that some of the children, while ravaged by the disease, came from homes where they were held, passed around to grandmothers, aunts and uncles, and other family members. The lethargic children were often products of teen pregnancies or came from severely poverty-stricken homes where the children had to fend for themselves while parents eked out a bare existence. He said those children were severely depressed and many would die even after receiving proper medication. With two babies in my arms and six around my feet, my tears spilling on their heads, I asked why. "There aren't enough arms to hold them. They need to be held and we barely have staff enough to take care of their medical needs," he gravely replied. (We met several doctors and other professional people who gave up lucrative and promising practices to live and work in Haiti to help conquer TB, which is rampant. Because the country is still so primitive and there is no communication in the mountains and little villages, testing and treatment require much diligence and time.)

Often now, when I am holding my grandchild and kissing him under his fat little chin and in the wrinkles of his healthy body, I see the faces of those precious Haitian children, ravaged by disease and malnutrition, and I hear, "They just need to be held."

I wonder how many children in our own country are suffering from "skin hunger"? I asked my daughter-in-law one day if she minded the way we passed Ryan around so much, hugging and kissing. She had just finished reading several books on child development and she said, "No, you are feeding him for me. I am the only one who can nurse him but he has 'skin hunger' too and you are satisfying that."

If it is absolutely necessary for you to work outside the home, it is also absolutely necessary for you to get a mother substitute to care for your baby, preferably a relative who will really love and want to hold and show unconditional acceptance and affection. I would also urge you to let a few other things go during the first six months so you will have time just to hold, love, and enjoy your baby. You can never go back and do it over, and affectionate parenting at this time will certainly give you valuable dividends later on.

Level 2 Love: Reality Parenting

This is the phase in which the parent replaces idealistic dreams with the reality of what the child is and a visualization of what he is becoming. This is an extension of the nurturing stage, and it lasts a long time, from infancy through adolescence.

How well does Level 1 love fare when that sweet infant shatters your image by refusing to nurse at the offered breast, choosing rather to scream with colic night and day? What about the realization that your child may not be perfect due to some allergy or abnormality? What about the realization of your imperfection at handling these new situations? What if this is your second child and the three-year-old begins to show signs of hyperactivity, and reverts to bed-wetting and thumb-sucking?

How well does Level 1 love hold up when you discover that through this long stage you are so attached to the child you hardly have an identity of your own?

Unfortunately, Level 1 love, while normally innate, doesn't hold up too well under these and a thousand other circumstances. While the actual love in your heart doesn't change, the practical, every-day-dealing-with-life kind of love needs some teaching.

I was puzzled at first by that portion of Titus 2:3–5 that says the older women are to teach the younger women "to love their children." It wasn't until I began to study child abuse that I began to understand. Whether you are loved or abused as a child has a lot to do with how you are trained to deal with your own children. It is especially necessary for an older woman who has some experience and knowledge to provide teaching if your home experience has been faulty.

During the infancy-to-six-year stage, many mothers suffer from a rude awakening into the sheer hard work and lack of feelings of individuality connected with caring for their children. Often they feel they have to have something else and they go to work. Mothers are surprised that the wonderful feelings of Level 1 love aren't

sufficient to sustain them through years of sibling rivalry, stubborn
potty training, and being almost eaten up by children who are more
takers than givers. With proper training, this stage can be a happy,
successful one, but it must be experienced in reality, not fantasy.
Because we are not offered any official courses in this kind of
training, we must search for it through good books, tapes, church
classes, seminars, and pastoral counseling. The greatest source for
you young women may be an older woman who has successfully
raised her children. Don't be afraid to ask her how she did it. It
might be a very rewarding compliment to her for you to ask her
advice about raising your children.

Leaving children during this age is often the easiest thing to do,
but it is wise to stop and count the cost. There were times when
with three children and a full-time, high-pressure job I would be
pushed nearly to the brink. It was then that I felt trapped for life,
helping Mark with homework he cared nothing about and Mike
with eye exercises and keeping little Mandi's fingers out of the light
sockets. I felt my insides flying apart from pressure and frustration,
and had I not been taught self-control, I might have hit and hit
until it all went away. I recognized early that there is a very fine line
between self-control and lack of control, and parents who really
love sometimes cross over that line and abuse their children, much
to their regret and shame.

I am certainly not saying here that working mothers are more
abusive than non-working mothers. But if the experts are correct in
saying child abuse is taught, isn't it time we took Titus 2:4 literally
and believe that we must teach younger women how to deal with a
life that is swarming with little people?

Dr. Fontana says in *Somewhere a Child is Crying*,

> I . . . believe that each community must take upon itself the respon-
> sibility for providing more and better day-care services, more and better
> training, and higher pay for child-care workers, more temporary shelter
> facilities, more lay therapists and parent aides and foster grandparents
> and homemakers. And I would certainly encourage the establishment
> and support of new chapters of Parents Anonymous.[8]

Is it a statement of our times that last on the above list of needs for the prevention of child abuse were *homemakers?* I would put them at the top of the list because I believe the rise in the outside employment of women has led to an unbearable burden on mothers to be too many things to too many people. Statistics reveal that child abuse has grown proportionately to the rise in mothers out of the home.

In commenting on the fallacies concerning the working mother, Linda Burnett states that a housewife would have to be blind and deaf not to have been influenced by the propaganda aimed at the "poor housewives" who don't even "know how unhappy they are"! But she says that some of the N.O.W. leaders are teaching women how "bad off" they really are in being at home—that it is "limiting, boring, lonely, and distasteful." As if that isn't enough, they say it is "meaningless."

> To get this message across, however, some myths have been created to make the exodus plausible, even preferable, to the instinctive priority we ascribe to being wives and mothers.[9]

Dr. James Dobson, in talking about one of these myths, vehemently disagreed that

> most mothers of small children can work all day and still come home and meet their family obligations, perhaps even better than they could if they remained at home. Nonsense! There is only so much energy within the human body for expenditure during each twenty-four hours, and when it is invested in one place it is not available for use in another. . . . Few women alive are equipped with the super strength necessary at the end of a workday to meet the emotional needs of their children, to train and guide and discipline, to build self-esteem, to teach the true values of life, and beyond all that, to maintain a healthy marital relationship as well. . . . To the contrary, I have observed that exhausted wives and mothers become irritable, grouchy, and frustrated, setting the stage for conflict within the home.[10]

What about day-care during this stage? Is it really harmful? Yes, says Dr. Paul D. Meier, unless there is at "least one well-adjusted, warm, loving staff member for every three or four toddlers."
Ms. magazine reported:

> Since most for-profit centers do not enroll federally subsidized children, they are governed only by the state licensing codes. These state laws are designed to protect only a child's health and safety. Depending on the state, they allow 10 to 20 children to be cared for by one teacher or staff member.[11]

In The Unwanted Generation, surveys and research conducted by several groups into 45 day-care facilities in Atlanta are cited, and the story is the same: the facilities are "unbelievably inadequate, crowded, dark, with poor or no playgrounds." The Washington Monthly reported that "most do not meet the widely accepted standards. . . ." The Child Welfare League estimates that 77 percent of available childcare spaces are inadequate and should not be used at all.

The Soviet Union has taken another look at day-care and has "noticed an astounding reversal by the government, from praise for their fifty-year-old day-care system to concern over the possibility that day care causes 'deprivation of psychological stimulation' and 'one-sided or retarded development.'"[12]

Among the facts that Linda Burnett sees concerning day-care are these: "Your child may suffer some degree of loss of identity. . . . Peer pressure stifles a child's individualism. . . . Your child's social behavior may be affected now as well as later on in life. . . . Affectionless character may result from mother-child separation."

> Early studies emphasize what John Bowlby terms "affectionless character," which is the impairment of the capacity to form and maintain deep and lasting relationships.
> Interestingly, many studies of childhood and adolescent backgrounds of criminals revealed either a complete lack of or poor mother-child relationships. The "affectionless character" from inadequate maternal

care is most likely the primary factor causing the capacity in criminals to commit atrocious crimes seemingly with no conscience whatsoever about these acts.[13]

After reading case histories of Lee Harvey Oswald and Charles Manson, I found that, while hating what they had done, I was overwhelmed with the sadness of their neglected, loveless, affectionless lives. As the crime rate rises and the atrocities become more and more brutal, I have to ask myself the question, "Who is the monster?" Boston Stranglers and Jack the Rippers aren't born, they are made; and the mold they are poured into during the nurturing stage is most likely to expel into society a perfect cast.

At the opposite end of the spectrum is the home suffering from lack of discipline. In one home the parent is the tyrant and in the other it is the child.

In learning how to love our children it is essential that we learn the proper attitude, method and timing of discipline. The proper attitude must be love. We must believe, and the child must also believe, that we are correcting him because in the long run it will be good for him.

The method? While Richard Farson, author of *Birth-rights: A Bill of Rights for Children*, advocates the elimination of spankings, the Bible clearly teaches that there are times when, as the old saw has it, the "board of education needs to be applied to the seat of learning." Proverbs 29:15 tells us, "The rod and reproof give wisdom: but a child left to himself bringeth his Mother to shame" (KJV).

When a child is too young to understand reasoning and discipline of another order, spanking needs to be administered in love. When parents let a situation continue until the pressure builds into full-fledged anger they are in danger of provoking wrath. "And ye fathers provoke not your children to wrath; but nurture them in the chastening and admonition of the Lord" (Col. 3:21).

While often more difficult to administer physical discipline when children are small and cute, it is easier when they become sassy, awkward adolescents who anger us quickly. However, if a child is properly disciplined before the age of five or six, he will be more easily dealt with from then on.

Working mothers must find a happy balance. Too many are lashing out unfairly and abusing children because they live at a pressure-point anxiety level all the time. Others don't discipline, either because they feel guilty using what little time they have left in that manner or because they are exhausted and they just hope for the best. This is not true of working mothers only; there is plenty of abuse as well as lax discipline going on behind the curtains of stay-at-home mothers too. I know there have been times I have just not wanted to discipline because I was tired or for various other reasons.

When Matt was four, Marvin and I worked at a summer training camp for teens. We swapped our teaching times and caring-for-Matt times. One afternoon, while I was studying in the kitchen, I heard a knock at the front door. There stood the camp director holding a wriggling, wet boy who was supposed to have been napping in the next room. Matt had slipped out and joined five-year-old Clint in surveying the swimming pool, where he fell in. Fortunately, the director happened by in time for a heroic rescue. Questioning Matt about the rule of never going to the pool alone, he sniffled, "But I wasn't alone; Clint was there."

As I looked into that cherubic face glistening with tears, I came up with a host of reasons for not punishing him.

1. He was *soooo* cute and such a baby still.
2. Maybe he *really* thought having Clint was enough.
3. He was *frightened already.*
4. He had *suffered already* by falling in.
5. He was *usually* an obedient child.

As I wrestled with "to spank or not to spank, that is the question," God brought a verse to my mind, and I read it to Matt: "Foolishness is bound in the heart of the child but the rod of correction shall drive it far from him" (Prov. 22:15, KJV).

I explained his foolishness to him and that God intended me to obey Him just as I intended Matt to obey me and that I had to spank him so that he wouldn't be foolish next time. I got a switch, because I believe that is what God meant by a rod. After the spanking he turned, grabbed my legs, and buried his face in my skirt. I picked him up and told him how much I loved him. He nodded his blond head and the air was cleared.

I too, learned valuable lessons from experiences such as that. Often we *think* we know where our children are but in reality we don't. This part of loving carries through all levels of parental love. We *must* have the time (whether working or not) to be in constant communication to know where our children are:

1. *Physically.* I'm sure you've heard the public service spot on TV, "It's eleven o'clock. Do you know where your children are?"

Not only does it show respect to the parents and provide them with information needed for peace of mind, but I believe *knowing* where your children are assures *them* of your love. As long as children live in your home, they should be required to let you know where they are going and when they will return. At our house, the rule varies with the age. Small children report almost hourly when outside playing and are not allowed to go off their street without permission. Teens must ask permission to go out and must be in by eleven o'clock unless they phone. After high school, they are required to let us know where they are and are expected in at eleven-thirty unless other arrangements are made. They have squawked and sometimes broken the rule, and they have been dealt with. I think for a parent to lie awake, sleepy and worried, shows irresponsibility of both parent and child. Someone has to teach it.

2. *Mentally.* Do you ever ask your children what they think about a particular subject? For example, "What do you think the writers of that program were trying to say about teen runaways?" "What is it you like about that recording artist? Do you think the way he lives is coming through in his songs?" Are you brave enough to ask them what they think about church or God? If you don't communicate often, you might be very surprised to find that your child is forming dangerous opinions directly opposite yours. We need to discuss in an interesting way books that we wish our children would read. Rather than saying, "Here, you need to read this—it will help you," this might be better: "Will you read this and tell me if this is the way young people really think now? Maybe I don't understand

what this writer is trying to say. Will you read it so we can talk about it?" What you are really saying is, "You are important and I value your opinion."

Not long ago, I heard a child, previously almost legalistic in his Christianity, say to his mother, "Mom, just tell them you are sick and that's why you missed the meeting."

"But that's a lie, I overslept!"

This opened up a long discussion on how the boy's thinking had changed. He had picked up some situational ethics and humanistic attitudes from somewhere. Rather than jump down his throat, she calmly showed how this thinking can creep in and change everything one stands for.

3. *Socially.* Children need guidance in choosing friends. For many years unselfish parents may have the privilege of providing the setting where proper friendships may develop by inviting families to visit which include children best suited to the molding of your child. In my opinion, children should not just be sent out to play with whatever children happen to be in the neighborhood, with no parental knowledge of the family. In many apartment complexes the new breed of "latch-key children" are free to become dangerously involved with harmful children as well as adults. I am reminded of the tragic death of so many black children in Atlanta and Chicago because parents for the most part didn't know where their children were physically or socially.

At first, I never questioned my children playing with children of members of our little church because I knew the parents. But during one period when Mark was thirteen I noticed that the more he was with one boy the more sneaky and rebellious he became. I put the FBI on it (Family Bureau of Investigation), by listening on an extension phone when this boy told where and when Mark should come to share a six-pack of beer and a pack of cigarettes. Wow! All the same day!

Yes, I understand about human rights and privacy and all the rest, but I also know I am like a lioness when it comes to protecting my young.

Mark sauntered into the kitchen to ask if he could ride his bike to the YMCA. Biting my tongue, as quietly as I could, I said, "No, honey, not today." He punched the familiar button and out came: "I can't *ever* do anything. I'm the only one who *always* has to stay home. *Everyone* else is going. I don't want supper anyway." Etc., etc.

During family devotions that evening we had a general discussion out of Proverbs about the pitfalls of the wrong companions. "He that walketh with wise men, shall be wise; but a companion of fools shall be destroyed" (Prov. 13:20, KJV).

Mark looked as if he thought that God had truly given us a divine message, and he had sense enough not to argue. Later I told him how I knew, and it was some time before he really understood. The other boy has not only been involved with heavy drinking and drugs, he has broken his mother's heart by marrying and divorcing, leaving his children with her. Now he has married a much older woman with children of her own.

While Mark was studying for the ministry, during his first sermon he made reference to the incident. "I'm glad I had parents who cared enough to help me choose my friends and to help me break up harmful friendships, even though I was not mature enough to understand at the time."

Did the other boy's parents love him? I know for a fact they did, but perhaps they had not been taught Levels 2 and 3 love. Reality love teaches that children are born sinners and like sheep *will* want to go astray. It is our duty as parents to be shepherds and pull them back from danger. It is not fun, and children hate it at the time. Some parents want to be popular at the wrong time. Often I have said, "I wish I could be your friend, but right now I have to be your mother." Recent polls indicate that my popularity is rising, especially with those who have left home.

Raising your own children and learning to love them on all levels is often a lonely and private affair, because each child is like a snowflake born into obscurity. There is not a certain pattern to follow, but during the obscure years before your child's "coming out party" it is up to you to preserve the uniqueness and individuality of that snowflake, fragile as it is. You must teach, love, discipline, nurture in such a way that the little snowflake can one day march out on his own, join up with other snowflakes and find his way in a responsible, productive, stable, and caring way.

4. *Spiritually*. All children start out in the same way spiritually. They are all lost and in need of the Savior. The most important thing a mother can do for her child is to lead that child to a saving knowledge of Jesus Christ and that at a very early age. Then, we *must* continue to know where they are spiritually. What is being taught in your child's Sunday School and is he or she understanding it? What programs are offered for growth—Good News Clubs, AWANA or Pioneer clubs, youth groups, etc.? Family devotions provide the ideal place to find out where children are through friendly, nonthreatening discussions. Don't punish them for having formed wrong viewpoints.

Level 3 Love: Acceptance Parenting

This is perhaps the most difficult parenting stage, since it deals with teenagers. Just at a time when you have spent about twelve years nurturing them, feeding them with food, philosophies, spiritual truth and traditions, they are overwhelmed with an avalanche of peer pressure and hormonal fall-out. You are ready to sit back and see if what you put in will stay in, only to be rudely jarred by the fact that they are rejecting your philosophies, traditions, and everything else but food. And now you read that you need to accept them during this time.

You are very likely to be in direct competition with everyone else in your child's life at this time, but if you understand that this is the way it is, you won't be hurt by it quite as much. About all you can offer now is guidance as you accept his individuality and temperament. You will have to be very skillful as you help him recognize his strengths and weaknesses.

This was a very frightening time for me as I watched our teenagers seem to throw off much of what we believed in and stood for, much like a too heavy overcoat. Many times I was afraid they wouldn't have sense enough to know what they would need. But, I have lived to see two of them step out into the cold night air just long enough to sense the need for that warm overcoat of values and truths.

I really believe if we do our job right, we will see our youngsters come back of their own accord for their warm duds. Most will try the whimsical, flimsy, trendy fashions, but they soon see there's no substance, no warmth or security there. Parents make a big mistake in overreacting when they realize they have not produced clones of themselves.

We can't control everything in the lives of our children, but we are expected to use our influence in the following three areas to insure that what we believe and teach our children is not being torn down in some other area.

1. *Home.* Home is the first church, the first mission field, and the first spiritual training ground your children have. Real Christianity must begin here and be lived out here consistently if children are to be strong, stable Christians.

If the children whose parents are the "pillars" of the church are falling away in the numbers reported, do we blame the church? This is not an indictment of anyone, but from some of the people I talk with, I hear something troubling. "Oh, sure, we look like the model Christian family at church. But we don't live it at home. It's a joke. The devil is in control of our home."

We have lived in three towns where there were Christian colleges, and this is what I hear most: "We left our home to come here to prepare for the ministry because my husband said God called him. I am cooped up with sick kids all winter while snow piles up round my door and bitterness piles up in my heart. He leaves before the rest of us get up to go to class and comes home just long enough to eat and tell us, 'You should have heard so and so. What a blessing!' Then he goes to work until midnight when he eats again and sleeps till morning without seeing the children. He doesn't even know what goes on in our world or the real world in general. I have had enough and I want to tell him to jump off a bridge!" What many of these dear students don't seem to know is that they may learn how to build a super church but they know little of building a home. I wonder how many talented preachers will never be pastors because their homes broke up while they were attending seminary

or Bible college? Even if the home survives, the children may cause
heartache and shame.

> And thou shalt teach them diligently unto thy children and shalt talk of
> them when thou sittest in thine house, and when thou walkest by the
> way and when thou liest down and when thou risest up" (Deut. 6:7,
> KJV).

That commandment was given to Israel with the admonition to
keep it that it might be well with them and that they might increase
mightily. It came right after the well-known command: "And thou
shalt love the Lord thy God with all thy soul and with all thy
might" (KJV).

Somehow it seems that loving God in the right way will naturally
spill over into the right love and teaching for the family. Day-care
can't do that, Sunday School can't even do it. The only place that
command can be obeyed is the *home!*

Beverly LaHaye quotes from Solveig Eggerz's article "What
Child Care Advocates Won't Tell You" (*Human Events* May 20,
1978), commenting on child psychologist Selma Frailberg's book,
Every Child's Birthright: In Defense of Mothering.

> The child who spends most of his waking day in an environment of
> indifference is a likely candidate for what Frailberg calls the disease of
> non-attachment, which is frequently incurable. These children grow
> into the "hollow men" of society, persons who, in their most harmful
> form, wander lonely and indifferent through life, and in the worst
> instances may be capable of blood-curdling crimes without a prick of
> conscience. Once a child is several years old, the chances of reversing
> this development are slim.[14]

Family devotions are still very important during this level of
loving, but as children grow and their needs change, you must be
willing to change to meet those needs. We have had to change
from after breakfast to before bedtime to right after dinner. We
sometimes have had three different levels of devotions going on.
Flannelgraph stories are for the youngest, with little workbooks and
topical and subject discussions for the older children. Like most

families, we have struggled many times in having devotions at all. Children who are very active with school, church, jobs, and sports are hard to catch.

I firmly believe that home must be the main attraction for children. While I love privacy, and after twenty-four years of having children around, I do get tired, I still want this to be the hub of all their activity. That means refreshments for gatherings and messes to clean up. It means carpets that are seldom clean and furniture that wears out before its time.

Home is the place where children learn how to appropriate their faith into everyday living by watching how parents do it. How I react to a rejection letter teaches my son or daughter how to react when overlooked by the coach. How we react to a disappointing progress report teaches them how to deal with those who disappoint them—even me. How their dad reacts when the car breaks down or the plumbing backs up teaches them how Christ is relevant for day-by-day reality.

Certainly an unattended home is not the proper place for children to gather at this stage any more than it is at the younger stage. If you work, chances are that much of what should take place in your home will have to be handled elsewhere. It takes a mighty special mother who can surround herself with her children and their friends after a hectic day in the checkout lane of the grocery she works in. You may want to list some ways your home is suffering because of your working. Perhaps you and your husband can make some changes.

2. *Church.* Before a child enters school he should already be regularly attending Sunday School and church. He should not just be dropped off but taken with the family. Before a child understands doctrine or theology, he can obtain much strength and comfort from the fact that his whole family worships together. If father doesn't go, it is vital that the female factor fill in here without nagging or making the father feel guilty.

Before I resigned from my job, one of the easiest things to neglect was church. Evenings were so precious that sometimes I felt it was more important for me to be with the children at home. And when you get up early every day, Sunday morning to just "lop around" seems like such a treat that you find yourself manufacturing aches and pains in order to indulge. Are your children in danger of being cheated out of valuable lessons to be learned at church because "you just can't do everything" now that you are working?

Be sure you know what the church is teaching. We left a denomination shortly after my conversion because there wasn't a strong emphasis on the Bible. We also left a good church that Marvin and I loved in order to attend another because it had a good youth program. It was worth the sacrifice. The teaching our children received from that church and the strong youth program that kept them occupied as well as spiritually instructed helped to make them the strong, committed Christians they are today.

Where I once judged churches by color scheme, I now know that, when children are involved, the most important phase of the church is that which sees to their needs. I have watched friends of mine who were Christians stay in a dead, liberal, modernist church because it was more socially acceptable. I have also watched many of them lose their children. A good Bible-teaching church is no guarantee, but it is at least a step in the right direction. Peer pressure is such a strong force during this time that we as parents would do well to provide ample opportunities for our children to be with peers who will press them into the right direction.

3. *School.* When I went to public school it was run much like Christian schools today, with dress codes, the pledge to the flag, Bible reading, and prayer. I have many friends teaching in public schools today who are fine Christians, and I *do* believe we must continue to fight for better public education. But there came a time when we felt that the school was tearing down those true values that we were working so hard at home and church to build. It was a very soul-searching and sacrificial decision that we could ill afford when we decided to place our children in Christian school. We realize that Christian schools are not perfect because our children are not perfect. But they have cooperated with our home and church in building principles, values, and morals, not to make children fragile, "hot-house" Christians, but to give them what it takes to operate in the real world. While they are young and tender and easily influenced, they are taught in a protected environment.

It is a fallacy to think that placing your child in Christian school will solve all your problems. You must take an active part in building and keeping your schools the way you want them. If the public schools are in a mess, who is to blame? I believe parents stopped fighting and demanding excellence, and I also believe this has been a sickness ushered in on the heels of women making their exodus from the home.

It seems that the only mothers who have time to be room mothers and P.T.A. presidents and members are non-working ones, and they are becoming scarce. When was the last time you looked at the textbooks assigned to your children? If you felt there should be some changes, would you have time to go to the school to fight for them? When was the last time you just dropped in at your child's school to see what goes on in the halls?

Some weeks ago while having a long conference with one of my children's teachers, I apologized for bothering him so often. I was surprised to hear him say: "I would stay here around the clock if I could get parents in to discuss their children. I have called some parents four times and still they say they don't have time. They are really expecting more out of the classroom than is possible. I really appreciate you coming."

Whether you choose private or public education, please contribute to the system by your concern and by your involvement. A school will be only as good as parents insist.

During this level of loving, your child will most likely gravitate into fields that interest him. Whether that includes sports, music, or farming, he or she needs support and encouragement and this also takes time. Does your working permit you to help develop your child's interests? Or does everything seem to revolve around your job and what you have time for? We at least owe our children an introduction to and an availability for extracurricular activities that interest them.

While Levels 1 and 2 seem to last forever, they aren't usually fraught with huge, heart-rending problems. Level 3, however, seems to fly by, but the flight is sometimes so turbulent and rough that you wonder if you will ever land safely. Perhaps you are in this stage now and can identify with the times I paced the floor, wringing my hands and asking, "Dear God, where have I failed?" Take heart, it is too early to judge success or failure. You are just in the "getting through it" stage. Believe me, you will one day look back into your memory album and chuckle. While the theme song for your home is "The Fight is On", I would like to sing you another entitled, "Hold On, My Child".

During this phase, while working is perhaps not as harmful to the children as in the earlier phases, it is the hardest on the female factor emotionally. If you can manage to keep the nest together and hold onto a career *and* keep your sanity, you don't need anyone telling you how to do it. I think you must keep your antenna high, your priorities straight and your heart tuned to God's will, your husband's desires, and your children's slippery needs.

Level 4 Love: Extended Parenting

This can be an unexpected time of joy if the other levels have been taken care of. It can also be the beginning of a life of heartache if you have made too many wrong choices during the other three levels. This is the period of time when you have done all you can in raising your children, and your love now extends to college and the people they will choose as friends and marry, to jobs you would rather they didn't have and philosophies foreign to your own.

This level is much easier physically and mentally because there are fewer people waiting in line for the bathroom and fewer hormonal imbalances occurring at the same time. But you can become an emotional basket case if you aren't able to sweep their corner of the nest clean. We must understand things are different than they were twenty years ago. If you overreact to people they relate to or ideas they are expounding, you may drive them farther away.

I have been trying to encourage a mother with a wayward son to keep the door open to him by loving him with this kind of love. The last time I spoke to her, in Florida, she said she had run into him at a mall and "He had *three* earrings in his ear. I just wanted to turn and run the other way!" We all have our breaking point. Hers was *three earrings!* What's yours?

While I agree that it's best for the smaller children that this boy should not continue to live at home while involved in activities that are harming him, I still believe that mother must keep the channel of communication open.

I encouraged my friend, "Next time you see him, don't presume that three earrings means being gay and don't run. Smile and take him out for a soft drink and ask him what the significance of the earrings is. You know, if he manages to get one hundred earrings dangling off that tiny earlobe, he is still your son. He may have added one more earring to test just what would make you stop loving him. Look beyond the hair, dirt, and earrings and try to visualize him as God wants him to be. Continue to see him that way while you pray for him."

There are hundreds and maybe thousands of testimonies by children who tell of being pulled back home and back to God by strong cords of love that defy understanding. It has been interesting for us to see one of ours come full circle—from radical ideas to a quiet conservatism that puts God first.

This is the level of love that actually does more than free the fledgling from the nest. It also frees the mother hen to become a peacock.

I tell a story that I heard about a little girl visiting her grandmother on the farm. While feeding the chickens, she was surprised to see a peacock. Running into the kitchen, she said, "Grandma, Grandma, one of your chickens is in bloom!"

Now is your time to bloom, female factor. If you have spent the first twenty years of your life being molded and deciding on the rest of your life, you may have just completed the next twenty years being involved in affectionate, reality, and acceptance parenting. You may now be entering into extended parenting in your early forties—full of experience, wisdom, and, hopefully, humor. You may need a brush-up course on something, but deep down you know you can take on the whole world and it feels good.

I am aware that the bulk of this chapter deals with Level 2 love because basically this book is a call to the only one who can truly nurture a child back to the nurturing station, the home. But it's more than that. Because the female factor who cooperates with

God during those long years when children appear to be her appen-
dages, comes away with her coffers full. She will carry into whatever field she chooses, a confidence of a job well done, an emotional security, and a deep feeling of pride.

Young mothers, how are you to love your children? In her new
book, *I Am a Woman by God's Design*, Beverly LaHaye says:

> Psalm 113:9 talks about the "joyful mother of children." The term
> *mother* in the Hebrew relates "to the bond of the family"—the one who
> binds the family together. How necessary it is for a mother to learn to
> love her children, so the family might reap the results of her love. [15]

I am not an authority on the sublime art of mothering, but am
looking and learning from every source available. I wouldn't dream
of showing up on a tennis court one day all dolled up in a tennis
outfit and announcing, "I'm a tennis player." Not until I have
learned how to play tennis and then practiced and practiced will I
actually be a tennis player.

In much the same way, mothering must be learned, developed,
cultivated, and practiced. No one expects you to be perfect, but
very few mothers who really give their best towards raising children
fail.

9. How Do You Spell Relief? W-o-m-a-n!

> A capable, intelligent and virtuous woman, who is he
> who can find her. . . ?
>
> Proverbs 31:10, AB

I found her, I found her! That is what I feel like shouting when I hear the question asked by this chapter title.

Statistically speaking, women read more books on family and marriage than men do. That is true of me also. But I believe so strongly in what my wife is trying to say within these pages that I wanted to get my two cents in. Even if the husbands won't read even this one chapter, perhaps it will be an encouragement to women to know that while most husbands (even me until now) will never verbalize how they feel, what you are doing in maintaining the home is vital to their lives.

Marilee explained to me that, while one of her goals of this book was to encourage young women to choose the career of keeper at home, she also wanted it to be a tool to help older women teach younger women, as set forth in Titus 2. She let me read her chapters on how to love the husband, the children and even the obey-the-husband part. When I asked her what she planned to teach women about being "good," she grinned and said she planned to leave that out. Knowing that she was struggling with feelings of not

131

being qualified enough to teach this subject, I asked her if I might do so in this chapter. Having received her permission, I'd like to share here the picture of a "good" wife as I see her portraying it.

A quick look into the dictionary at this common word *good* revealed some interesting brief definitions. They describe a "good" wife including mine: "Suitable to a purpose; efficient; beneficial, valid, genuine, real, honorable; worthy, dependable; reliable; above average; adequate, satisfying, morally sound or excellent; virtuous, kind, generous; well behaved, dutiful, proper, skilled," to name some.

No wonder Lemuel's mother, who gave us the teachings in Proverbs 31, said a woman that fit that description is rarer than precious jewels.

Now, while my wife admittedly has faults and weaknesses, she generally fills the bill of being "good" in the marriage relationship as well as in the role of a mother. In very simple terms, I want to tell you what that means to the *keepee*, me.

When God said that it was not good that Adam should be alone, I know what He meant. I for one had to have someone to share my life with, and though I had very little instruction on my role as husband, I jumped in with both feet some twenty-five years ago. In *The Husband Book* Dean Merrill says:

> It's not surprising that you are in many ways a chip off the old block. After all, you started life with his genes. You are biologically similar to him. None of us knows how profound and far-reaching are the influences of fundamental heredity.
>
> And you spent the first eighteen or so years of your life—the most impressionable years—watching him. It would be highly unusual if you *didn't* copy him—subconsciously—in the many details and decisions of being a husband. . . .[1]

I watched my dad all right, and I determined not to be like him. (Now deceased, he was an alcoholic who rarely provided for his family.) Until my stepfather entered my life in the teen years I had no male role-model, and the home life I observed left much to be desired. I knew my wife came from a more stable home but other than that and the sheer love I had for her I had nothing else to go on. I don't know if I even knew what I wanted back then, other than just her. But I know now, I think, what most men want. A man wants a wife because she completes him and gives him something to live for, to love and come home to; someone to work hard and accomplish goals for. No matter how successful or how macho a man may appear, it is the female factor that gives him the total feeling of being a man.

Since my wife quit her job some fifteen years ago we have had the agreement that I would provide the income for the family and she would care for the children and keep our home a haven from the outside world. Many times I have been made aware that she has perhaps the most difficult job. One such time was when she was left totally blind and incapacitated with multiple sclerosis. I found myself not only with my job but with total responsibility for four children—their clothes, meals, and emotional upheavals—and a home badly in need of a woman's touch. I tell you, my prayers were intensified after a few days that lasted eighteen hours and ended with me falling asleep folding diapers. I just didn't have what it took to do it like she did. Not only do I pity the men who are increasingly finding themselves in that situation permanently due to divorce, but I also pity the woman who is working and keeping the home as well. It takes a superwoman.

Recently some men were incredulously asking me how I managed after twenty-five years to have such a happy marriage and home, especially in light of my heavy travel. I explained that although I enjoyed all my jobs, whether selling or estate planning that I now do, I didn't enjoy being away from home. However, the old adage "Absence makes the heart grow fonder" does have much truth in it.

There was a time that lack of communication about the travel issue caused us trouble. Marilee thought I purposely took traveling jobs to avoid being at home and assuming responsibility as a parent. I had no idea she felt that way, because we weren't communicating well at the time. When we finally did communicate, I explained that I found it difficult sitting in an office doing the same thing over and over, and I naturally gravitated to jobs that don't require this. When she understood this and I understood that when I arrived home she might be weary from all the responsibility, we began to work to solve the problem. A strange thing happened when we removed the anger and began to seek ways to make each other happier. For example, after that when I would come home full of good intentions to take her away from the house for a nice dinner, it would be only to open the door to wonderful aromas emanating from the kitchen. Knowing that I had eaten out for every meal she had prepared my favorite dinner as a special welcome-home treat. That just set the tempo for me looking for something to do to please her. I look forward to getting home mainly because I know she is there.

I appreciate that Marilee has always taken herself seriously in the roles of wife and mother. She has been there to love when I wanted to love. We have always tried to go out on a special date about once a month, often overnight. We believe that getting away from the house routine, our noisy children, and the doldrums of my job has kept our love fresh and our friendship growing. I really look forward to that date and the time away. It gives us a chance to look back and remember how far God has brought us and to be grateful for the blessings. It also gives an atmosphere in which to dream about where we are going. The dates we have had on a regular basis all these years have meant more to me as a husband than anything I could tell you in print.

Every man, I believe, should make a point of taking his wife out at least once a month, if possible. The relaxed times of sharing lead naturally into a most satisfying physical relationship.

These times keep the walls of anger from forming or getting too high. They keep the flame of love from getting too low, and they give you time to talk over things that are difficult to discuss at home.

These times have also given me a chance to obey God's command in 1 Peter 3:7, which says husbands should "dwell with them according to knowledge." The Amplified Bible puts it this way:

> In the same way you married men should live considerately with [your wives], with an intelligent recognition [of the marriage relation], honoring the woman as [physically] the weaker, but [realizing that you]

are joint heirs of the grace (God's unmerited favor) of life, in order that your prayers may not be hindered and cut off.—Otherwise you cannot pray effectively.

I believe if God said we are joint heirs that means my wife and I are equal in God's eyes and that I had better dwell with her according to knowledge. Women seem adept at knowing their men, but God had to strongly advise the men to "get to know your wives."

The trips we have taken have helped me find out how my wife thinks, what she likes or dislikes, what makes her laugh and cry, what motivates her, and what discourages her.

Lack of knowledge led me to be insensitive to her needs when I moved us so often. Once I understood how it made her feel, "Like a bird ripped out of her nest," I determined, unless absolutely necessary, I would not move her again.

Lack of knowledge about her love and talent for cooking caused me to be so reticent in trying new dishes. After countless times of turning up my nose over anything new and different, we had a lengthy, if cool, discussion about why we didn't eat the same thing over and over. I decided that if she loved me enough to spend hours in a hot kitchen creating gourmet delights for me, the least I could do was try them. I was surprised to find I had been missing out on some wonderful things. That she serves fantastic, beautifully prepared meals, on an attractively set table makes mealtimes a real treat for our whole family. The setting she provides invites us to warm and often important discussions.

Dwelling according to knowledge means taking off the masks and being honest. Admitting that I was wrong in that area gave me a unique opportunity to teach the children that this admission isn't a sign of weakness but strength. Honesty (while it hurts sometimes) blesses your partnership and draws you closer together in Christ, creating greater love and understanding.

I am well aware that I am where I am today to a large degree, personally and professionally, because I have a wife who does me "good and not evil all the days of her life" (Prov. 31:12, KJV).

She loves and wants nice things but acknowledges that money is hard to come by and therefore keeps me out of bankruptcy court by not demanding the biggest and best of everything. I'm well aware she has been willing to drive whatever car happens to be left over and during the poor years refused to drink juice so there would be plenty for the rest of us.

She has contributed to whatever I was involved in by opening our home to my friends and business acquaintances, offering them good food, clean beds or just plain hospitality.

I've seen her hopping mad when someone maligned my integrity, fighting to protect my reputation and I'm grateful.

Knowing that I'm to be the spiritual leader, she has willingly stepped in to fill that position whenever I had to be gone.

She sees to it that I am dressed to suit whatever project I'm involved in. I don't worry about her leading me off into an embarrassing situation.

Like a mother hen, she has insisted and pushed me to doctors when I would have let things go, like a tumor or numbness in my leg.

She puts me on a diet when she sees the threat of a heart attack looming over my spare tire. She chides me into running with her.

She is always attractive, warm, and responsive when my arms long for her.

Whether she does it for me or herself, I appreciate her taking such good care of "my girl" by keeping her hair neat and her figure trim (most of the time). I also love the fact that a good portion of her wardrobe purchases are cute nighties.

I'm glad that I have confidence that she will do her part of raising the children just the way I want her to.

We realized a long time ago that Satan will destroy any marriage he can. Because he is the prince and power of the air, he can just stand aside and let husband and wife destroy themselves as he introduces pride, jealousy, bickering, selfishness, indifference and no willingness to pull together to make a marriage work. The hot, exciting love that zaps you in the heart when you first meet is not enough to carry you through the years of changing and hard knocks with family and business. We discuss our differences (sometimes loudly) and even argue, but we also try to help each other in our weaknesses, keeping the one goal in mind: We want this marriage to last and we want to enjoy it.

We are coming to the dessert time in our lives soon when it will be just the two of us again. The world system prodded by overactive media will have done its best to split us up; children will have worn us thin but we will have survived. We vowed to continue making our love sweet and strong, to enjoy life together and even traveling together when the children are all gone.

I think the thing that makes my wife a good keeper at home is because that is what she chose to do. I am aware I'm married to a woman who could do many things but who refused the call of a career in order to put *us* first. There was a tremendous spiritual truth in that for me. Just because we are capable of doing a thing doesn't give us the green light to do it. Through that knowledge, I've learned to submit to God's will for my life. Many calls each year offer me opportunities that could make us wealthy. Every year I turn down jobs that would more than double my income in the ministry. I know I could do a good job too, but God, in giving me the ability to do many things, also gave me a choice. Do I do what I want or what He wants? Male or female, in fact, that same question applies: Do I do what I want or do I do God's will?

We have observed many of our friends become two-paycheck couples. Some have waited until their children entered school, but others took the step even before. Whatever their reasons, changes have been evident that we don't want.

1. Their financial independence seemed to alter their attitude. Each partner gave off an aura of "I don't need you any more." I agree that marriage shouldn't be built on need, but it is a blow to the male ego to suddenly be without a reason to work so hard.

2. They go their separate ways. Their days off and vacation periods don't coincide, so they take separate vacations.

3. Home becomes a convenient stopover where people eat what they want when they want, come and go without any consideration of the family as a whole, rather than the happy, congenial place where Marilee and I spend three-quarters of our time.

4. Mealtime is not the only time to suffer; sex suffers.

5. They develop separate friends rather than making friends with

couples; then their separate interests divide them at a time when reinforcement is needed.

6. They are often falling in love with someone they see in a more favorable light and with more frequency.

Certainly, I'm not fool enough to say the years of diapers, colic, measles, Little League practice and dirty floors were exhilarating for her. But perhaps when Paul said, "Notwithstanding she shall be saved in childbearing" (1 Tim. 2:15, KJV), he meant that through motherhood she found deliverance from the very frustrations that were built into her lot as a woman in our fallen world.

I think the following verse is the key to my wife's being a "good" keeper. But then I think it applies to me too: "For whosoever will save his life shall lose it: and whosoever will lose his life for my sake shall find it" (Matt. 16:25).

It would appear that the woman willing to lose her life temporarily in the lives of her family stands to gain the most. God's economy seems backward to us—lose in order to gain, give in order to get and die that we might live. But it works.

As I see it, for me to have a "good" wife, I must love her as Christ loved the church. Now, that is quite an order. Christ, after all, died for the church. And if that wasn't enough, He came to life again to sit at the Father's right hand and He is *ever* making intercession for His bride. I must love my wife in that manner, being willing if necessary to die for her, but in the meantime being willing to live for her and *ever* keeping my heart tuned to her needs.

How do you spell relief for the heartache that is crippling our families? WOMAN! That's it—men must be men and allow the woman to be what God created her to be by providing the necessary tools: a home, finances, moral and emotional support and lots and lots of understanding love.

10. Is Chastity Still in the Dictionary?

Virtue has more admirers than followers.
Countess of Blessington

If you ask a group of teenage girls what chastity means, they'll probably tell you, "That's the name of Sonny and Cher's daughter."

To answer the question—yes, *chastity* is still in the dictionary and it means "virtuous, not indulging in unlawful sexual activity."

Let's look at another question: Who is chaste? That may be hard to determine but, according to Johns Hopkins University professors Melvin Zelnik and John F. Kantner, nearly 50 percent of the nation's 10.3 million young women age 15 to 19 have had premarital sex.[1] The percentage has nearly doubled since Zelnik and Kantner began their surveys in 1971. These figures reflect answers given by those willing to admit their sexual activity. Judging by the girls who drop out of Christian schools due to pregnancy, we can assume that not every girl in a Christian school is a virgin.

Where did chastity go and who is responsible for its demise? While I admire two senators who recently introduced a proposal to spend federal money "to promote self-discipline and chastity," I don't know that federal intervention is the answer. I agree with what Utah's Senator Orrin Hatch says: "When young people engage in intimate physical relationships before they are ready or willing to take the responsibilities of marriage or child-rearing, they jeopardize their own emotional or physical health."[2]

I also agree with the proposal's pro-family emphasis as drafted by Senator Jeremiah Denton. This would turn centers now being used to help girls get birth control devices or abortions into centers to "promote self-discipline and chastity and other positive family-centered approaches" in order to reduce adolescent pregnancies. Denton says, "No nation can survive long unless it can teach its young to withhold indulgence in their sexual appetites until marriage."[3]

For Janice, a fifteen-year-old sophomore interviewed on a TV talk show in Tampa, Florida, chastity was helped out the door by a working mother who had little time for discussion or supervision. Janice recalls how she was swept up into the exciting but scary world of adolescent hedonism. "I just couldn't handle the pressure anymore. I wanted to become part of the gang and when I did, I also became part of what they were involved in, partying, hanging out, cruising and drinking. Having the house to myself every afternoon didn't hurt. I was urged to have sex with my boyfriend and did but it was a real downer. I knew my parents wouldn't approve but it was important to be part of the group. Everybody was doing it."

While sociologists, educators and parents may be aghast at the pleasure habits of the young, they view it in retrospect as the fallout from the decade's great social upheavals. They believe the numbers of sexually active young women are climbing due to the following: (1) women's liberation; (2) the divorce rate; (3) the decline of parental and institutional authority; (4) the widespread acceptance of "living together"; (5) the swift media treatment of these trends.[4]

The message everywhere is sex, and the sexual revolution spawned as a social protest on college campuses of the '60s has filtered down to junior high and high schools. Not only are children reaching puberty earlier than ever, they have fewer restraints. They take their cues from a pleasure-at-all-costs society and are playing precocious sex games while parents are at work.

Actually the absence of parental guidance is somewhat like taking a fence down to let sheep find grass in whatever pasture at whatever cost or danger. Some of the dangerous jutting cliffs and poisonous weeds our children are exposed to come in the form of rock music, TV, movies, and reading material. The poison is offered and the little lambs are eating it up, with no shepherd to interfere. Sex is packaged and promoted and taken for the norm in all of these areas. One jeans company, for example, pitches its contour-explicit pants by picturing scantily clad teens astride one another. In teen music, such tunes as "Take Your Time (Do It Right)" and "Do That to Me One More Time" stay high on the charts for months.

Provocative films like *Porky's, Private Lessons,* and *Foxes* exploit sex among the young. TV programs are no less exploitive of this trend.

Once chastity was something to be guarded—or lied about when lost. Now an uncommonly virtuous teenager lies to protect the dirty little secret that she is still a virgin.

What price freedom? What are the results so far in this promiscuous, partying culture?

Before we look at our own country, let's take a look at a country that preceded us in the sexual freedom race by about ten years—Denmark. Is it true that more and more sexual knowledge, freedom, and permissiveness will lead to fewer unwanted pregnancies, sex-related crimes, and lower venereal disease statistics? Let's consider the "disaster in Denmark":

1967—Legalization of pornography;
1970—Sex education made compulsory;
1973—Abortion on demand was legalized.

The results speak for themselves in urging America not to follow their lead:

1. Assault rape increased 300 percent!
2. Venereal disease in ages over 20 increased 200 percent!
3. Venereal disease in ages 16–20 increased 250 percent!
4. Venereal disease in persons 15 and under increased 400 percent!
5. Abortions went up 500 percent!
6. Illegitimate pregnancy went up 250 percent!
7. Divorce rate went up 200 percent!

These statistics from the 1977 Statistical Yearbook of Denmark, as quoted in the Sex Education and Mental Health Report published by Christian Family Renewal in 1979, leads us to believe that the porn kings are lying when they say more pornography in print and on the screen will lead to healthy sex lives. Supporters of sex education claim education is the answer to venereal disease and unwanted pregnancies. If education is the answer why are the abortions up? I believe that chastity is the answer and that we are obligated to do something to cure our own personal and national illness.

1. Teenage pregnancies are epidemic: a million teenage girls— one out of every ten—get pregnant each year. Statistics in a 1977 study show that 600,000 unwed teenagers were giving birth each year, with the sharpest increase among those under fourteen.[5]

2. A great many of the million and half abortions performed each year involve a teenager.

3. Venereal disease is rampant among adolescents, accounting for the 25 percent of the million reported gonorrhea cases each year.[6]

Recently the topic of genital herpes was discussed on the *Phil Donahue Show* by two patients and a doctor. The program, while distressing, was informative.

This disease, caused by a virus, with no known cure, is contracted through sexual relationships. It seems that once you have it, you have it for life. According to the experts, there is no age, race, or economic distinction, with some patients in their late sixties and many others young teenagers.

There are now groups to provide the support of group dynamics to herpes victims as well as groups for the representing of still another special-interest lobby.

I listened to Phil Donahue's guest and callers discuss the open sores that recur sometimes monthly but at least a couple of times a year and the problem of whether or not you tell your next sexual partner he or she might contract it. By the end of the program, I was disturbed—severely disturbed—that the solution to this epidemic problem is merely information to be disseminated to the millions affected. The experts kept reassuring the audience that having herpes was not because you were "bad" nor as punishment for your behavior.

I was reminded of a verse of Scripture: "Woe unto them that call evil good, and good evil; that put darkness for light, and light for darkness, that put bitter for sweet, and sweet for bitter" (Isa. 6:20).

The young male patient's closing message was, in effect: get informed, yes; learn about your bodies, yes; but don't be frightened. His exact words: "Still, go out and have a good time."

Where are the parents who should be shouting—the cure for herpes is abstinence?

"Whatsoever a man soweth, that shall he also reap" is proving true in reality. It has always been true, because it is the word of God.

God is certainly not to blame for the spread of herpes, but I believe it is just one more judgment against sin that people who insist on free sex are heaping upon themselves. The other venereal diseases have also been adding victims at an epidemic rate.

4. Emotional complications ranging from extreme disillusionment to guilt, anger and deep depressions are increasingly common. A clinical psychologist at an adolescent treatment center in New York expressed the opinion that sexual activity before age sixteen or seventeen is counterproductive because of the immaturity of the emotions of younger adolescents. In her studies, she found that most younger girls had not enjoyed their sexual experiences. Emptiness was also a frequent reaction to the lack of ongoing relationships in their experiences.[7]

But who is responsible for all this gloom and doom? What can we teach young people about sex and who can teach them?

I also recently heard a young man being interviewed who claimed to be asexual and had taken a self-imposed vow of celibacy. I *might* trust him to talk to my daughter about chastity. But I can't think of many men, other than her father, who could handle it. Men are experts at helping women and girls get rid of their chastity, but I believe it is the female factor's responsibility to help them keep it. Of course kids experimented with sex long before the great exodus by mothers from the home. But it wasn't so easy.

Just being home is not enough, however. Mothers need to pre-pare themselves by understanding as much about human sexuality as possible and by being honest in the discussions. Keeping lines of communication open with teens is almost a mystical experience, but it is vital in sexual instruction. That must begin early with the mother initiating discussions in an unembarrassed manner so that the child feels open to talk to mom about everything.

With all the new uproar about sex education in the schools, we are finally seeing what twenty years of sex education, free con-traceptives, counseling, abortions, explicit films, and all the rest have produced. The experts say those of us who oppose these things are afraid of knowledge. What are the results with the kids who have had the knowledge handed to them on a humanistic platter? The above results show that the problems have not been alleviated but have multiplied. If knowledge is the cure, why are we not closer to healthy sex attitudes? My answer is that sex education without Biblical values is not much more than a "how-to" course.

For the young woman, chastity must be taught at home by example and discussion. If that is not possible, an older Christian woman should at least be available in every church to give guidance and instruction—modern instruction, that includes the teaching that God views sex as good.

There are so many good books on the market now that the Christian woman has only herself to blame if she remains ignorant. Since this chapter doesn't pretend to be a sex manual or to be comprehensive in covering the subject, I would recommend begin-ning with *The Act of Marriage* by Tim and Beverly LaHaye or *The Gift of Sex* by Clifford and Joyce Penner. Often I have sat down and discussed matters dealing with sex with my own children and I just want to share a few of those thoughts here.

1. There is no "free" sex, other than that within marriage. When a couple keep their bodies pure for each other and go into marriage in that condition and stay faithful, that is "free" sex. You may pay for the whole relationship but you don't pay for sex. When you must pay for sex, you are either using the services of a prostitute or a gigolo. If you are jumping in and out of bed with those generous souls who give it away, you can be sure you will eventually come away with something to remember them by.

2. God made sex for not only procreation but for pleasure. "Let thy fountain be blessed; and *rejoice* with the wife of thy youth." (Prov. 5:18). Study the Song of Solomon closely.

3. Did you know that Christian couples enjoy a more satisfying sexual relationship than non-Christians? In *The Act of Marriage*, the LaHayes reported the following findings of a survey:

a. A Christian's relationship with God produces a greater capacity for expressing and receiving love than is possible for a non-Christian. The fruit of the Spirit, (love, joy, peace, kindness, etc.—Gal. 5:22 and 23) removes the specter of resentment and bitterness that devastates an exciting bedroom life.

b. In addition, people who genuinely love each other will strive harder to please one another, become better informed, and treat each other more unselfishly. This will naturally enrich their love life.[8]

If that's not good enough, how about a *Redbook* survey that confirmed that the "strongly religious woman seems to be even more responsive than other women her age." The reason seems clear: if a woman really understands the Biblical teachings on love-making, she will suffer few inhibitions and openly enjoy her husband's expressions of love.

Not only is the keeper at home responsible for the house, but she is also responsible for the youngsters who live in that home. She must not be backward in teaching her children the right way to live. There is a right way regardless of what the "experts" tell us as they lead our children down a primrose path of destruction.

I tell my children if they will be open and honest with me we will talk about *anything* and I promise to not be shocked. That promise has at times been hard to keep, but I believe that our children have healthy, normal attitudes about sex. Rather than just curse the darkness of "sex on every corner," we have chosen to use it as a teaching tool. In fact, advertising of feminine sanitary products opened the door for discussion sooner and easier than it might otherwise have come.

I *am* slightly offended by the blaring advertisements for such personal products that women must know about and use. However, if you will jump on a soapbox rather than cough nervously during discussions or scenes that might embarrass you, you might find some interesting object lessons. For instance, on the *Phil Donahue Show* recently, guests representing what they call sex-for-fun playthings, from mail-order adult items to adult book and film shops, made the statement that "Sex isn't love; sex is for fun and games." Had one of my children been there, I could have asked, "What do you think is wrong with that statement?"

It is important to remember that you were once young, and perhaps you can bring that into the conversation. "I understand how you feel. It is hard to be different when everyone is doing it."

Martin Luther wrote to a young man trying to decide the question of marriage:

> Chastity is not in our power, as little as are God's other wonders and graces. But we are all made for marriage as our bodies show and as the Scriptures state in Genesis 2, "It is not good that man should be alone; I will make him a help meet for him."[9]

Elisabeth Elliot says in *Let Me Be a Woman:*

> God did not limit the gift of sexuality to those who He foreknew would marry. But the gift of sexual intercourse He ordained exclusively for those who marry. This is unequivocal in Scripture. There are no exceptions. Intercourse without total commitment for life is demonic.[10]

Mrs. Elliot warned her daughter of the privacy and intimacy of the inner sanctum of human knowlege—sex.

> Beware of the how-to-do-it books. There is danger in analysis. You can't learn the meaning of a rose by pulling it to pieces. You can't examine a burning coal by carrying it away from the fire. It dies in the process. There is something deadly about the relentless scientific probe into the mechanics of sexual activity—the lights, cameras, artificial organs and instruments, the note-taking observers and the horrifying detailed reports published for the world's delectation. . . .
>
> George Steiner wrote, "Sexual relations are, or should be, one of the citadels of privacy, the night-place where we must be allowed to gather the splintered, harried elements of our consciousness to some kind of inviolate order and repose.

The new pornographers subvert this last vital privacy; they do our imagining for us. They take away the words that were of the night and shout them over the rooftops, making them hollow. The images of our love-making, the stammerings we resort to in intimacy, come pre-packaged. . . . Our dreams are marketed wholesale."[11]

It's a wonder that poor, uninformed couples like my husband and me ever managed, let alone enjoyed, sex. But then, what of our parents and theirs before? Can it be that the telescope into our bedrooms and the magnifying glass looking for every erogenous zone have clipped the wings of the bird of mystery? I'm not against knowledge, and understanding my sexuality has been helpful, but I believe sex is a journey begun with marriage (studying the map before), and with each passing year, new territory is to be explored. With each plateau of emotional and spiritual growth there comes a new awareness and capacity for enjoyment of each other's bodies.

Who is responsible for teaching the young women in your house chastity? You are. As your daughters watch your relationship to your husband you can be sure a picture speaks more than a thousand words. The tender touching and warm embracing throughout the evening with the family will let them know that there will be more to follow in the privacy of your room. Many parents behave as if they would *never* do *that!* Thus, kids go elsewhere for their informa-tion—to someone who knows about *it* firsthand.

It is up to you and your mate to *show* your children an alternative to what they are seeing in technicolor now—that marriage is good and fulfilling and, most importantly, worth waiting for.

II. What I Save by Staying at Home

> It is not education which makes women less domestic—
> but wealth.
>
> Katherine Gallagher

My excuses for not working outside the home are wearing thin. By current logic, I should rush onto the overcrowded highway every morning with millions of other coffee-primed women who believe they must go to work to stay ahead of inflation and/or achieve the nebulous fulfillment.

My children need me. Do they really? For all intents and purposes two are adults and on their own; one is in college and one in junior high.

How about *My skills are outdated?* Courses in sharpening career tools and career alignment are offered at every junior college, college and even adult high schools.

Sometimes truth *is* stranger than fiction. Except that that is what I want to do, my real excuse for remaining a keeper at home is that what I save by not working is more valuable to me than what I can earn. The more I thought about it, the more examples I came up with. They fit into three main areas of practical saving and living: (1) money (that's right, we actually save money by my choice of remaining a homemaker); (2) relationships; (3) health. Let's look at them in some detail.

148

MONEY

That day fifteen years ago when I marched into the office and gave up the job I loved I also gave up nearly half our income with one arrogant thought: "God, this is your idea, so you'd better take care of us." I didn't mean to sound sacrilegious, nor was I an expert on the promises of the Bible, but I had heard our pastor teach a lesson on Philippians 4:19: "But my God shall supply all your need according to his riches in glory by Christ Jesus." What impressed me was that the pastor said God's reputation is at stake when we trust him; and God promises to supply *needs*, not *wants*.

Another promise I clung to was James 1:5, 6: "If any of you is deficient in wisdom, let him ask of the giving God [Who gives] to every one liberally and ungrudgingly, without reproaching or fault-finding, and it will be given him. Only it must be in faith that he asks, with no wavering—no hesitating, no doubting . . ." (AB).

Arming myself with trust in God's promise of supply, and asking for wisdom to make the most out of what was provided, I tried to sort out my wants from my needs. This spilled over into teaching the children the difference between the two. "Yes, dear, I know you *need* tennis shoes, but you just *want* Adidas." We did need a car, but we didn't need a new one. We all wanted a color television but realized that wasn't a definite need.

Teaching those values to demanding, often selfish children is not easy and certainly not fun. During those years, if a Worst Mother award had been given, my children would have voted for me. "*Everybody else* has Adidas! . . . We're the *only* family in the world who rides in a beat-up old station wagon and watches a black and white TV." From time to time they suggested I go to work to provide them with some of extras they wanted. But in the long run, the lessons they have learned by not having everything they want-ed, by trusting God for everything from a tennis racket to a scholar-ship, has prepared them for a life in a time when the American dream is in the fast lane, headed the wrong way.

From a tax standpoint, marriage definitely pays off for a one-income couple filing jointly (or in a case where one partner has a great deal more income to report than the other). For today's growing ranks of dual-income couples, marriage is a costly proposition.

To illustrate the tax benefits for a one-income married couple, consider your husband earning $22,000, while you have no income and you use the standard deduction. Your joint-filing bill comes to $3,219. A single person has to pay $4,517 on exactly the same income, so in this instance you save $1,298 by being married and not working. The savings grow along with your taxable income.

What happens to the couple who earn $22,000 apiece? Sounds great, doesn't it? How does a tax tab of $11,086 sound? That gives you $10,914 take-home pay if you have no other deductions. Let's consider a hypothetical choice a woman in this salary range must make. In the *Two-Paycheck Marriage,* Caroline Bird tells of "Mrs. X," a suburban wife of a $15,000-a-year executive and mother of one. Desiring to return to work, she refuses a $15,000 industrial biologist job because of the long hours and pressure. Another job, college teaching with more flexible, shorter hours, but less pay, $10,000, is considered. Of that, let's see what she would keep.

Day care	$2,400
Wardrobe	1,000
Modest lunches	500
Commuting	600
Dry cleaning	500

Mrs. X totals her estimates and finds that family expenses will increase approximately $5,000 if she returns to work. Yet her employment will not provide the family with any new deductions or exemptions. Her very first dollar of income will effectively be taxed at her husband's highest rate. His taxable income is $8,000 so her first dollar will be taxed at 22 percent. Her employment will therefore increase the family's federal income tax bill from $1,380 to $3,820 (1972 rates); her share of the bill is thus $2,440. Assuming state and local income taxes averaging 5 percent, her cost is $500. Social security tax amounts to another $468 (1972). Mr. and Mrs. X calculate that Mrs. X's gross income will yield a net of $1,592.[1]

A woman responding to a *Better Homes and Gardens* survey said that so much of our money is given away to support people who wouldn't work that many women who didn't want to work, had to. She said a woman should stay home and raise her family, calling that the "most economical and intelligent way to support family life."

It appears that a woman would be well advised to stop and count the cost of her liberation from the stove. You may, as I did, find it wiser to save my pantyhose, stoke the home-fires, cook a pot of homemade bean soup and enjoy the home we work so hard to have.

This brings up another area of extra cost when you work—food. I found that when I worked, a good portion of what I earned went to pay for convenience foods because I was too tired to cook from scratch when I got home. Considering my love of cooking, I felt that not only was I cheating my family by spending more on less nutritious foods but I was also cheating myself out of one of my most enjoyable and creative efforts.

Here is where the wisdom of God really comes into play. With proper planning you can serve nutritious, interesting meals at a minimum of cost, without waste.

Our old freezer has more than once paid for itself through bulk buying. I buy an almost endless variety of breads at a discount bakery store. At five loaves for $1.49, compared with $.89 per loaf at the grocery, we have a savings of $2.96. (Freezing restores moisture to old bread and most towns have a day-old bread store.)

Buying weekly meat specials in quantity for the freezer gives variety, top quality, and low cost. Every couple of months one supermarket in our area has whole, semi-boneless hams for $.89 per pound. I usually purchase two, have them cut (for free) in half, securing about four thick, center slices for ham steaks and breakfast ham. Packaged center slices are well over two dollars a pound.

Perhaps chicken or turkey is the next week's special buy. If you could ever sock away an extra hundred dollars to put my plan into practice you would find that you don't have to pay the premium dollar for premium meat. You can get especially good buys in beef by getting a whole loin or round and having it cut. Often I get ground beef that sells packaged for over three dollars a pound for $1.59 by buying the whole cut.

Using newspaper ads to learn your markets, you may find, as I have, that certain stores have lower prices on regular items. When in their area, stock up on those items. For instance, one store has about twenty items that are much cheaper than the competitors, although they are higher on everything else. This store always has one major brand of cake mix for thirty cents less than the other markets.

Perhaps the thing that takes the biggest bite out of the working mother's check is running to the grocery whenever she has to at night or on Saturday, buying on impulse or in a hurry and paying top dollar for everything. I feel I save at least twenty-five dollars a week by shopping carefully and comparatively. Again, I have time on my side.

Learning the art of couponing and refunding can bring tempting new foods into your home that you might not otherwise be able to afford. We save refund dollars in a special envelope, and when we have enough, we go out to a nice restaurant for dinner.

Once when a supermarket was offering to triple the value of manufacturer's coupons, I received $38.00 back after paying the $90.00 grocery bill. I *always* stock up on detergent, toilet paper, facial tissues, beauty products, and coffee when one market has double-coupon day. If you have time, you can take part in triple-plays, that is, using a manufacturer's coupon on an item that also either is marked down by the store or has a newspaper coupon of its own. After that double savings you are able to send either the label from the product or the cash receipt for more coupons or a cash refund. Susan Samtur, author of *Cashing In at the Checkout*, once rang up a bill of $130.18 and paid only $7.07 after giving her coupons to the cashier. Such savings won't be realized on every trip, but Samtur says the careful shopper can easily cut bills in half by using coupons and refund offers consistently.

U.S. News & World Report reported that more than 80 percent of U.S. families now use cents-off coupons. With almost every item priced over a dollar now, this makes good sense.

It does take considerable time to clip, categorize and shop, using coupons, and if you are working, it will be doubly difficult unless you can get the family involved. Our kids are so into it that they automatically ᵗake the labels and boxtops off containers. I find satisfaction in thinking I'm beating the system of inflation by not spending one unnecessary nickel. It is one of the ways I earn the extra benefits I would gain by working.

I don't know whether I am prodded by the starving-children-in-China stories heard in childhood or if I am just a tightwad, but I can't bear to waste food and I've developed methods of using every scrap. Every week I cook my major meat purchase of ham, beef roast, or turkey, from which I get two main meals before I slice the best remaining portion for sandwiches. I wrap these in small packages and freeze them, leaving plenty of chunks and small bits for ham or turkey salads and casseroles. Especially tasty in the winter months is the bean soup made with the ham bone—Great Northern beans and heavy on the garlic. As well as being rich in protein and less than a dollar for the whole family, it simmers all day and frees you to work at some other project.

I keep a "potpourri" jar in my freezer in which I layer all the little tads of leftover vegetables with their broth, along with meat scraps, gravy, and rice. When the large, colorful jar is full, I thaw the contents, add some tomatoes, and presto—an almost free vegetable soup. Again, low in price, low in time, but oh so good.

Many of the meals I prepare that whittle down the cost of food would be nearly impossible if I worked until five o'clock. Picking the meat off a turkey carcass for a casserole is for the birds when you can pick up fried chicken at a deli, but that triples your cost per serving. I pack lunches, using the frozen sliced turkey, ham, and beef for sandwiches that would also be more than triple the cost if picked up at a deli. Add that to the price of one of the twenty-four cupcakes I get out of my $.58 cent cake mix and some carrot sticks, and you can see that those home-packed lunches are not only cheap but they are eaten instead of being tossed out like so many of the school lunches. I figured the price some years ago when all four children were in school and I saved nine dollars a week. It would be much more now.

Most food chains offer generic products ranging from canned vegetables to tea at 20 to 50 percent below the cost of similar national-brand items. Also, now popular are the "no frills" stores where people can economize by buying private-label brands and bagging their own groceries, and food cooperatives which buy in bulk. However, these too take additional shopping time so hard to come by for the working mother. If you can enlist the help of all family members by showing them what they could buy with the savings, you might be able to make a game of it.

Michael Jacobson of the Center for Science in the Public Interest, a Washington group, says consumers can save up to 25 percent a week on food costs. He adds these tips for more savings: (1) Pack your lunch at least a couple of times a week. (2) Eat less meat and more bread, potatoes, rice, fruits, and vegetables. (3) Drink more water and less soda pop, coffee, and alcoholic beverages. (4) Shop at farmers' markets. (5) Make better use of leftovers.

On Monday mornings, meat counters are a virtual garden of marked-down meats (still good but the color is not as bright). Look for cheddar cheese that has the beginnings of mold and ask the dairy clerk to mark it down. They often mark it in half and are delighted to sell it. All you have to do is scrape off the mold.

I don't believe God is pleased with waste while watching so many of His children going hungry in other areas, so I try to be a good steward with the money I'm allowed to have.

If you have a small plot of ground on which to plant a vegetable garden, it has been estimated that you can save $250.00 per year on vegetables and fruits.

Let's just add that amount to the $315.00 I would save on school lunches and the $1,200.00 I save couponing and refunding and you have $1765.00. Then compare that with the $1592.00 the woman would get to keep out of her $10,000-a-year salary.

That certainly does not take *everything* into account, and because of ever-changing inflationary factors is a very rough comparison. But it does point up some realities that need to be considered.

I also save money on clothing, household articles, and gifts by having the extra time to comb the newspapers and roam the shops. I suppose I deserve the label of hard-core-shopper since I don sensible shoes (the only time I do) and stand in the cold at the front door of the mall the day after Christmas looking for my Christmas gifts for the next year. By the end of February they can call me anything they want, but I have stashed away most of next Christmas's shopping, as well as 50 percent of the cost. I wouldn't dream of buying wrapping paper, Christmas cards, ribbons, etc., any time but the day after Christmas. The mainstays of so many Christmas lists—sweaters, robe and gown sets, belts, houseshoes, etc., are on their final mark-down in February.

Check your area for factory outlets. Families can cut clothing costs by 25 to 75 percent by trading at factory outlets, many of which handle name-brand merchandise. At a factory outlet for one chain in our town, ladies' blouses that retail for $25 to $40 sell for about $10.

In our part of the country furniture and department stores hold special sales around holidays. Try to put away some money and wait to shop until a sale is advertised. Thrift shops and outlets operated by Goodwill Industries and the Salvation Army offer good buys on furniture and appliances as well as clothing. Scouring the flea markets and garage sales can offer family entertainment as well as some real bargains.

It has been estimated consumers can save up to 40 percent by shopping by the calendar at seasonal sales. Nearly everything you need will probably go on sale at some time during the year. As a general rule, you'll save the most if you purchase things out of season or at the end of the season.

Make a list of the items you'll need throughout the year, including gifts. Buy them on sale and store them until they are needed. While I have had my own private calendar in my head for years, papers and magazines are now printing them. The following guide will help you know when to look for what.

January: The traditional white-sale month, with big discounts on linens and towels. Storewide clearance sales offer 50 percent savings on holiday merchandise, from Christmas cards and ornaments to toys and gift items. Other good buys include appliances, furniture, stereos, storm windows, and sporting goods.

February: Lincoln's and Washington's birthday sales and final mark-downs on January leftovers. Check out bicycles, dishes, bedding, air conditioners, curtains, glassware, men's shirts, rugs and carpets. Gardeners should check catalogs and start early indoor seeds to be transplanted later.

March: End-of-season sales on winter items as well as pre-season sales on spring clothing. Plan ahead and look for next winter's coats, sportswear and equipment. Other bargains may include china, housewares, laundry appliances, storm windows, and luggage.

April: After-Easter bargains abound in sales on women's dresses and coats, men's and boy's clothing, and pre-season summer items. Time to shop for building materials, paint, garden tools, wallpaper, and outdoor furniture.

May: Mother's Day and Memorial Day sales mark the time to replenish stocks of winter blankets, garden supplies, handbags, lingerie, tires, TVs, and towels.

June: Father's Day sales, plus end-of-semester sales on school supplies, including typewriters. Other potential good buys include cars, tires, men's clothing, hosiery, summer sportswear, frozen food, furniture, and fabrics.

July: Storewide clearance again. The biggest markdowns are usually near the end of the month but choices may be limited. July Fourth sales usually include bathing suits, shoes, air conditioners, outdoor furniture and sports equipment. Our best buys ever in furniture have been over this holiday.

August: A second round of white sales. Now is the time to buy summer clothing for next year as well as enjoy pre-season discounts on fall clothing.

September: Labor Day sales, back-to-school promotions. Final sales on garden supplies, outdoor furniture, and summer clothing. Good buys on china, glassware, furniture, bedding, and silver. Pre-season winter merchandise is offered. Season tickets are usually discounted now.

October: Sales on the last of old-model cars, as well as Columbus Day coat promotions. Take advantage of post-season sales on bicycles and fishing equipment and pre-season sales on ski items, electric blankets, and home furnishings.

November: Veteran's Day sales. You'll also find the lowest prices of the year on paint, hardware, and other home-improvement supplies, along with relatively good buys on blankets, stoves, water heaters, and used cars. This also is the time to look for bargain bulbs, shrubs, and trees for late fall planting. Try to shop early; the sales fade as the stores switch to full-price Christmas merchandise.

December: The very worst time to buy anything. This is the major month for retailers; reduced-prices and sales are few. If you have planned wisely, you should be able to avoid big purchases.

Proverbs 31 gives some of the activities of the ideal keeper at home. Among them are seeking wool and flax and developing them; seeking merchandise and food from afar off; she spins and sews and makes tapestries and rugs; she even sells garments that she makes.

All of those projects seem foreign to me unless I project what they *mean* into our lifetime. Some of the things I have mentioned so far deal with projects that *mean* the same thing. I don't spin or sew but I watch for sales that make it possible to have items for less than I could make them for. I scour the markets for the best, nutritious buys in food and take the time to prepare it well. In other words, while our life doesn't resemble the Proverbs 31 woman's life, in many ways the meaning can be the same. We must take care of the needs of our household.

Finally on the money topic are the savings derived by doing our own paper-hanging, painting, and yard work. With time, parties for children can be planned on the barest budget. Expenses for getting children to and from school and extracurricular activities result in a hefty sum too. If inflation continues we must master the art of outmaneuvering high prices.

With all the wisdom that God promises to supply us with to make the best use of our money and talents, we must not forget that what He is mainly trying to teach us is to trust in Him.

Our family lives in a town of seven colleges, one of them being a Christian college housing a seminary and Bible institute. One thing taught in these institutions of higher learning with emphasis on Christianity is that, whether preparing for the pastorate, the mission field, or education and business, you must *trust* God. *Trust* Him to lead you into the right area of ministry, *trust* Him to guide

you as you serve, and *trust* Him to supply your needs. The thing
that astounds me is that while these men are in class learning these
wonderful truths, they are sending their wives out to work to pay for
them to learn how to trust God. Why? "There is no way I could go
to school if she didn't work." It is rare to find a couple completely
looking to God to provide a way to earn the money needed without
always answering the prayer by sending the wife out to work. What
better place to put into practice the lessons learned in the
classroom.

Couples called by God to the life of faith have thrilling stories to
tell of God's supernatural supply so that mother doesn't have to
leave her children. Sometimes it involves part-time work of
babysitting, typing, or needlework. Sometimes it involves a
miracle.

RELATIONSHIPS

By being a keeper at home I save my relationships because most
are not suffering from lack of love *or* money but from neglect. It
takes mainly time to foster, nurture, and protect relationships.
Material gain aids comfort and ease but does little towards nurturing the soul. So many things are being written on how to have
"quality" time with your husband and children but few on the
spontaneous times. What happens to the child who needs to unload
his hurts or share his victories right after school or the husband who
can hardly eat until he gets "it" off his chest? Time cards and slots
seem to work well in everything but human relationships.

Love thy neighbor as thyself? Who is your neighbor? When was
the last time you visited other than when a death occurred?

While I don't actually have an outside-the-home job and bring in
a salary, you must know by now that I don't just get a thrill out of
bleaching my wash and buffing my floors. While maintaining the
over-all control of my home I also am busy speaking, writing,
counseling and teaching classes. While all of these are admirable
endeavors, I often find myself in the same perplexing situation the

working woman is in. Something has to go—I hung up the super-woman jersey, remember? It seems that relationships are the first to go, and I'm ashamed to list the order in which relationships suffer if I get too busy. I'm aware of many women so busy serving the Lord that they neglect the Lord's people.

Relationship with the Lord. This, sad to say, is the easiest relation-ship to neglect, because He doesn't put up a fuss. He just patiently waits until we miss Him so much we get back into fellowship. I think it is easy because we can't see in His eyes the hurt there. The old adage, "the squeaky wheel gets the grease" is true. After a period of "serving" without spending much time with the One I claimed to be serving, I was struck with the thought that God doesn't care as much about what we *do* as what we *are* to Him. He is our heavenly Father, after all, and we wouldn't dare hurt our earth-ly father by never spending time to talk with him.

How to make room for God in an already jam-packed day? Some-times it means getting up an hour earlier. But most often it just means realizing that, no matter what I have to do, it will be done more wisely and more lovingly the way He would do it if I seek Him first in my day.

Whether working or not, if it seems that you are being pulled apart by your responsibilities, you would do yourself a favor by making time for your heavenly Father. He really loves you and He just wants a few minutes of your undivided attention. If you will ask Him, I believe He will make a time and a way for you, so your day will run smoother and your nerves will be less frayed.

I am not suggesting that if you spend a few minutes each day in your Bible all your problems will be over. The quiet time with the Lord is not a magic wand to wave over your life. It is much more personal than that, a real relationship with a real person, the God of Glory. Withdraw to some quiet place, pull an imaginary curtain around you, and read God's love letter, knowing that He is speak-ing to you, individually and personally. If you read only one verse, meditate on it and try to see how you can make it apply to your day, you will have gained more from that few moments with God than you would from a whole course in college.

For instance, my favorite, Philippians 3:13 in *The Living Bible*, says:

> No, dear brothers, I am still not all I should be but I am bringing all my energies to bear on this one thing: Forgetting the past and looking forward to what lies ahead, I strain to reach the end of the race and receive the prize for which God is calling us up to heaven because of what Christ Jesus did for us.

That one verse, looked at in several translations and *applied*, for just that one day could change your life and the lives of those around you. In meditating and praying—talking over with God anything you want to in ordinary language—you may realize that you need to forget the hurtful remark your husband made and reach out to him with love. Perhaps you were passed over for a promotion and someone who wasn't as deserving got it. When you make up your mind to forget it and reach forth you will be surprised by the peace that is yours. Especially try to forget where you have failed and just ask God to help you not to fail there again. This washes away guilty feelings.

If you were to choose one verse a day that you could really chew on and apply to your life, at the end of the year you would have 365 verses in your heart and 365 changes in your relationship with the One who loves you most. There is no telling how many people during this time you would have influenced if you shared with them what you were learning.

Relationship with Friends. When I went to work a strange thing happened. I neglected my old friends but didn't know it because I was making new ones at work. On the surface, that didn't pose any problems, because I didn't actually think about which people were friendly acquaintances and which were true friends. It was when I quit work and began to live a different lifestyle that I learned who my true friends were. They were still there, left on a back burner but ready to resume our friendship, willing to bear with my changes. I heard a man say recently that if you could count four friends at your death who had been true, loyal, and forgiving you were most blessed. You put into a friendship much of what you put into a marriage—acceptance, forgiveness, unconditional love, sacrifice, and self-denial.

Some of the saddest verses in the Bible deal with friendlessness.

I looked on my right hand, and beheld, but there was no man that would know me; refuge failed me; no man cared for my soul (Ps. 142:4).

The impotent man answered him, Sir, I have no man, when the water is troubled, to put me into the pool; but while I am coming another steppeth down before me (John 5:7).

These verses are being repeated hundreds of times a day in varying degrees. Those of us who have chosen to be keepers at home can barely stay home because of the dear senior saints who need to be taken to the doctor, the grocery, or just out to lunch, because their daughters and daughters-in-law are working.

Being busy with an outside job has its advantages, like not having to face the people who are needy and hungry and whose souls need caring for. Sometimes I wish I could spread the salve, "I wish I could help, but I work," over my aching heart—aching because I don't have more hands, feet, and money. We are God's only instruments to carry out His work on earth, but I don't believe He meant for so much to be done by so few. Do you have time to be a friend to the friendless?

Something that bothers me is that long friendships seem to be going the way of long marriages. The minute a friend shows himself or herself to be human or fails us, we get a new one. "A friend loveth at all times," Proverbs 17:17 tells us. Old friends are like fine pieces of silver: they need to be protected, cherished, and polished often.

When younger, I wanted everyone I met to be my friend. That got me into trouble. ("He that maketh many friends doeth it to his own destruction; but there is a friend that sticketh closer than a brother"—Prov. 18:24.) We often confuse the need to be friendly to everyone with being bosom friends. It is impossible to be close friends with everyone we meet. But the Lord brings into our lives those we really click with and those friendships, while costly, are stimulating. "Iron sharpeneth iron, so a man sharpeneth the countenance of his friend" (Prov. 27:17).

They are also profitable:

Two are better than one; because they have a good reward for their labour. For if they fall, the one will lift up his fellow; but woe to him that is alone when he falleth, for he hath not another to help him (Eccles. 4:9, 10).

A true friend is so rare that next to the marriage relationship I believe it is most precious. "And Jonathan caused David to swear again, because he loved him, for he loved him as he loved his own soul" (1 Sam. 20:17).

If you must work, don't neglect your friends. There come times in our lives—news of cancer, death of a child, calamity or disaster—when nothing else matters except God, family and friends.

Neighbors. If I were to ask you to name your neighbors and tell something about them, could you? One scene I miss from my childhood is neighbors, gathered in yards, chatting and swatting mosquitoes in the summer evening. Before so many women worked and before television ruled our lives and schedules, our activities, and meals, you could see them in swings or hammocks, drinking iced tea, and sharing with each other.

I have a theory, perhaps unscientific, that psychiatrists' couches are filled with people who once could have been cured by "under the maple tree" therapy. Most people are crumbling because they feel all alone in the mess they find themselves in. Yesteryear, they would have heard, "Hey, don't feel so badly, the same thing happened to me. It all blew over in a couple of months. Keep your chin up." Millions of dollars being spent for professional counseling could just as well be saved if we had some neighbors practicing the ancient art of listening in the backyard.

I often wonder if I would have made a serious attempt on my life if I could have sat down with an older neighbor woman every now and then. If I could have poured out my fears about raising children, my anger over crippling illness, etc., she might have helped. I have a dear older lady living behind me now, and recently when I was not handling a problem very well, I told her about it. She confided that she had gone through the same thing twenty years earlier, and she gave me some wonderful advice. Now she peeks through the hedge and winks her moral support. I know she is there and she cares and that means so much to me.

Each person has a particular slot to fill in our lives, but working sometimes jams the slots with "Occupied" signs and our neighbors fade away into the clouds of busy activity. We need each other. Marvin and I see our own neighbors getting older and know there are many things we can do for them. I happen to think one of the things that pleases them most is our wanting their advice and opinions, acknowledging that they are still important to this system we are in.

If, during our sojourn on this earth, we are to learn something of love we must look at Christ's statement "Thou shalt love thy neighbour as thyself. There is none other commandment greater than these" (Mark 12:31) and Paul's injunction ". . . Let every one of us please his neighbor for his good to edification" (Rom. 15:2).

Neighbors are so comforting during sickness or death when they remember you with food or flowers and words of encouragement. When I worked I would sometimes find out a neighbor had passed away and been buried before I even heard of it. I couldn't have helped much anyway. The female factor, as it relates to neighbors, can be summed up in the following verse:

> Well reported of for good works, if she have brought up children, if she have lodged strangers, if she have washed the saints' feet, if she have relieved the afflicted, if she have diligently followed every good work (1 Tim. 5:10).

I am aware that a neighbor is not just one who lives next door, but anyone who comes into your life. That stretches the borders some and what God expects of us is not always easy but it is rewarding.

Distributing to the necessity of saints, given to hospitality (Rom 12:13).

Be not forgetful to entertain strangers: for thereby some have enter tained angels unawares (Heb. 13:2).

Husband Relationship. Most of what I wrote in the chapter on marriage is possible because I have the time to make it work. I know most men won't admit it, but they do become jealous of their wives' time and attention being aimed at anyone or anything else, unless they are constantly reminded that they are very important to us. We must be careful not to take this relationship for granted.

Relationship with Children. The main purpose of this book is the children: the children loved, but abused; latch-key children; the children who can never volunteer their mom for field-trip chaperone; the children who will run away today; the children who will commit suicide; and our children, yours and mine, who may never suffer any of the above but who may have confused values and insecurities if we don't put all we have into them.

Most of what I wanted to say I said in another chapter. Still I must say again that I find myself guilty of neglecting my relationship with my children if I am not very careful. Feeling as I do, I know many mothers who also must feel frustrated about their roles. Many children, having gone off the deep end into drugs, crime, or sex, say that no one would listen to them at home. They form relationships that strongly resemble families, however harmful they may be, because their peers treat them as important enough to listen to them. The most frightening of all families—the Manson family—guilty of murders and other atrocities, were very loyal and true to one another.

A key word that sums up what is lacking in relationships is *hunger.* Not many children in our country are physically hungry, but they, like husbands, friends, and neighbors, are *hungry* for those qualities that make a relationship—time for caring, loving attending, and just plain having fun. People tell me they can't remember the last time they laughed. How about you? Are you enjoying your relationships with God, husband, children, friends and neighbors?

If not, are you brave enough to examine the cause? Relationships that matter cannot be bought.

HEALTH

In my case, working a high-pressure job and trying to maintain my home too, led to numerous physical and emotional problems. Anxiety and guilt are worn by most working women like some sort of garment, and I was no exception. Migraine headaches became the natural outlet for me as I managed to be a super-achiever, if it killed me. Other friends of mine had ulcers, insomnia, and depression that had no cause other than the pressure.

Surveys reported by recent newspapers and magazines show that, while men have led in heart attacks, high blood pressure, and other stress-caused illnesses, the wide margin is narrowing rapidly and women are now as susceptible. Many women are running on amphetamines (to prove they have the stamina to keep up) and coming down on tranquilizers (because they must get their sleep so they can get up and run all over again).

I am aware some women, like some men, thrive on high pressure—that's what makes them tick—but I also think those women often try to speak for all women. Others feel pushed into the marketplace and haven't the emotional or physical stamina to handle it all.

Mothers who used to be home and could nurse their families through the various childhood diseases and flus are now out there catching whatever is going around, and no one can take care of anyone else.

Keepers at home who are well disciplined are in good physical shape. They have time for jogging, fitness programs, and getting out in the sunshine and fresh air.

I'm not aware of any statistics that prove whether the keeper at home is any healthier than the career woman. It may be some years before we get a clear picture. All I can go by just now is my own health and peace of mind. It is, after all, the peace ruling one's heart and life that produces an over-all feeling of well-being. As keepers we have to guard against boredom that can lead to anger and result in depression. Being creatively involved in church, community affairs, and future interests gives something to look forward to as well as training for future goals.

Science writer Maggie Scarf, in her book called *Unfinished Business: Pressure Points in the Lives of Women,* shocked feminists with her findings.

> Women are vulnerable to depression because their emotional attachments are much more important to them than to men.
>
> These apparent differences raise a troubling possibility: that emotional bonding, once a key to survival, is making women's lives more difficult in today's feminist era. Women are caught between the demands of their genes, urging them toward marriage and family, and a society sending them powerful new signals to be independent.
>
> The working women studies were just as depressed as those who stayed at home, reinforcing the unsettling conviction that mood is a function of biology. [2]

New York feminist Barbara Seamay charged Scarf with, "a seductive sellout of the feminist goals of greater autonomy for women."

Ruth Greenberg, a therapist at the University of Pennsylvania's Center for Cognitive Therapy, says *Unfinished Business* seems written "from a female chauvinist point of view. It makes depression look good, because it's a result of women's deep commitment to relationships, capacity for nurturing and greater sensitivity."

While the results of all the current hoopla are being tabulated, women would be best advised to do what we have been criticized for—follow your heart.

12. Express Your Magnificence

> And the king loved Esther above all the women, and
> she obtained grace and favor in his sight. . .
>
> Esther 2:17

I think the reason I love Esther so much is not that she was so beautiful and charming that the king chose her. It's not that she was clever in the way she got what she wanted out of the king, by wearing her best gown and standing in the right light. She employed all the old female tricks and could be passed off as just another dizzy dame—if it weren't for those five little words, "If I perish, I perish." That's when Esther expressed her magnificence! She was willing to give her life to save the Jewish people, their history, their tradition, and their relationship to God. Her uncle Mordecai, upon learning of the imminent destruction of their Jewish nation, went to Esther to plead with her to go to the King. Against her cry that it would be certain death for her if she wasn't received well, he said, "And who knoweth whether thou art come to the kingdom for such a time as this?"

You can read the entire story in the Book of Esther. The point I want to make here is that Esther had no idea what God was going to use her for. All she knew to do up until that time was to be a woman, the best woman she knew how to be. Perhaps she didn't even know she had it in her to say, "If I perish, I perish."

So much of what I believe is wrong with the confused, frantic search by women for self-fulfillment and identity is their failure to stop and look at God's overall plan and to recognize the neglect of their own magnificence. Still this failure is easy for me to understand personally, as I so often indulge in blind-man's-bluff. Like this morning.

A beautiful, warm spring morning greeted me through my Cape Cod curtains today. At first I was overjoyed to see the sun after a whole day of dark rain. But the joy was quickly pushed down as I gave way to anxiety over the monumental tasks of my day. I felt my stomach tightening as I lay in bed trying to decide what to do first. Some things, of course, don't take decisions—preparing breakfast, making lunches, cleaning up the kitchen. Those tasks often seem like leg-irons restraining me from more important tasks. I needed to catch up on correspondence, work on this book, do errands, get my clothes ready for a trip. But the book was the big problem. After all, isn't writing a book more important than all those mundane tasks that anyone could do?

I sat and did an anxious, legalistic devotional time while the gentle breeze seemed to be beckoning me to take a much-needed walk. After inner struggle about "wasting" thirty minutes, I decided to do my praying as I walked. I'm so glad I did.

Tiny crocuses peeked through the red sod and golden daffodils bowed humbly, reintroducing me to the overall plan. I recognized that I was "fretting myself," as Psalm 37 explains, and that I was being told, "Be careful for nothing; but in everything by prayer and supplication with thanksgiving, let your request be made known unto God" (Phil. 4:6).

I poured out my heart to God about the sheer sameness of being a woman some days. I told Him I was anxious—especially about the book—that I knew in my heart what I wanted to express, but it just wouldn't come together, and I felt pulled and pushed and I needed relief.

I got my relief and I also got a much bigger picture in truer perspective, as He gave me some insights.

The sun that had peeked through my window earlier had just been a teaser. I remembered that when I raised the shade, the room was flooded with light patterns that danced on the carpet. While God was in control of the light, I had control over the shade and it was ultimately my decision to let it in. How often we as God's special designs refuse to let Him lead us in His light while we stubbornly keep the shade of self-seeking pulled down on the windows of our soul.

Not once on my walk did I notice an azalea bush striving to shed its gentle, silky flowers in an effort to form more hardy dogwood blooms. While my tulips along the front walk have not bloomed yet, they were far enough along for me to hear if they had been grumbling about their boring routine of coming up year after year in the same spot with the same-colored robe. Rather, as I looked at the tulips that had already bloomed in a neighbor's yard, they seemed to say, "It is our ultimate fulfillment to cooperate with the Creator and Designer. Whether or not you came out to see and enjoy us, we are delighted to lift our heads to the Master Planner and bloom just for Him."

Like Esther, the tulips were willing to perish if that was the overall plan. Had I picked them and made a centerpiece for a dinner party, the perspective would have changed and they would have expressed their magnificence to more people. But they would still have been tulips.

Perspective changes both our view and our attitudes. Some view the world as being upside down now and some regard being a woman as an inconvenience or an "accident of sex." While I can't agree that we are born woman by accident, I do agree that it is sometimes inconvenient. I used to look up and down the pew at church when all four of our children were young and feel great pride and gratitude. But for me to enjoy that little scene took lots of inconvenience on my part: shopping, washing, getting up early, polishing shoes, and all the rest. But tell me, where in life can you achieve anything without inconvenience? There are limitations that define the gifts and abilities of every living thing.

The bulbs that are blooming have been buried and nearly forgotten for a whole year. They are breathtaking now as they express

their magnificence, but a limitation of time and environment is
placed on them. It is the very burial for an express length of time
that makes a tulip bloom.

Sometimes the overcoming of obstacles results in the birth of
something beautiful. While the freezing Virginia rains and snows
would push a camellia bush to its limit and kill it, the lilac thrives
on that very harshness. The lilac has been a favorite of mine since
childhood; while I lived in Alabama and Florida, I would have
done anything to grow lilac bushes. But I knew the limitations—
they must have cold winters and can't endure the long, humid heat
of the south. Whether I like that or not makes little difference. I
must adapt to that fact as well as to the fact that God designed and
made me a woman. That was His choice for my life. Rather than
lose the perspective of the overall plan and the ability to enjoy it, I
accept the limitations that are forming me into what God called me
to be. I cannot curse the soft curves and smooth skin that make me
feminine without jeopardizing the expression of my magnificence
when the time comes.

There is a time to plant and a time to harvest, and I find myself
between the two. I am in that state of having begun to grow and the
husbandman is weeding, caring for, and if need be, pruning me,
preparing me for that day when I shall lift up my head in His
presence and bloom according to my kind, to become what He has
planted. Yes, I hope to be lifted up, by my limitations, into perfect
union and freedom and into the will of God.

Christ's willingness to be our Saviour was limited to His willingness to die on a cross, bearing the sins of the world.

I was called by God to be woman. Even now, I would use my life
in nobler ways—to be broken bread for suffering humanity, to try to
point every lost soul to Jesus Christ—but I am limited by being a
woman. I am limited by the husband God gave me and by the
children spawned by our union. My limitations are mundane, not
glamorous or noble, something a scullery maid could do. But in
God's perspective, in the overall plan of things, what I am doing is
noble. It is accepting the gift and using it until He places another in
my hand.

Whenever Michael with his clear, strong tenor voice sings an operatic aria or a portion of a Bach cantata or just an old spiritual song, I feel like shouting, "He's mine; *I'm the* mother." But somehow the quiet, serene way he lives his life, trusting God, is more gratifying to me.

When I hear Mark preach or watch him play with his baby or open the door for his wife or hear him talking deep things with his father, I know we did a good job.

When we have listened to Mandi quote verses from the whole Book of John and Romans for her Bible quiz team or counsel her friends on the phone or heard her sing with her group, we've thanked God that He gave us the opportunity to watch a tiny child accept the Savior, and live her whole life for Him. Now, as a young stay-at-home bride, she has become more than we dared hope for.

I thank God that through the obstacles we've overcome we've learned a little more how to raise Matthew with even more enjoyment.

There is a tree outside my office window that has taught me some deep spiritual truths. When I first met this fifty-year-old tree it was fully clothed in lush, green leaves. It fits into the center of the window as if it were framed, and I loved the shade it provides. Having been in Florida for some years at that time, I had forgotten what fall could be like. As the season progressed, that tree decided to put on a show for me. The shadings on the leaves turned to vibrant yellow tinged with red. When the wind blew, a virtual ballet of color and light entertained me. It was as if the tree was aware that it was at its most beautiful time and was the subject of great admiration. It reminded me that there are times in my life when being a woman is beautiful, as on my wedding day when all the attention was on me, or when I held a newborn to my breast. I felt beautiful and complete then, almost mystical, and I tried to hang onto the feeling, knowing that somehow I was in touch with God the Creator as He allowed me to partake in creating. But this feeling passed and there were times when I thought God had made a mistake. It was for me as it must have been for the tree when its yearly time of glory had passed and the dry leaves fell, leaving it ugly in its nudity.

You can't create something without being limited by it. The

tree is now giving birth to new leaves, but they are just tiny yellow-green nubs. Barring a disaster, the leaves will turn into dark green toddlers and in the fall they will be colorful teenagers and when frost comes they will move out because they don't need the tree any longer.

One grey, monotonous winter day I talked to the tree rather honestly, pointing out how drab and ugly it seemed to be. It no longer provided shade or usefulness and could no longer entertain with breathtaking dances. But then I was reminded of the bare, ugly, useless times in my life—times when I thought there would be no more beauty, that my life was over. The Lord reminded me that that was what the resurrection was all about. "Except a corn of wheat fall into the ground and die, it abideth alone; but if it die, it bringeth forth much fruit" (John 12:24b).

There are many deaths in the life of a tree and in the life of a woman. I have faced the death of a young bride, young mother-hood, the tiny figure and wrinkleless face, and there are other deaths to come. Each death gives way to a resurrection of a new life, periods when we can start over. Perhaps my tree friend, sprout-ing his little nubs, is thinking just now, "I'm glad to have another chance. This year I will have more leaves and provide more shade and wave to more people. I will be a better tree, for you, Lord." Then I benefit from that.

Certainly there are bare, ugly times in our lives. The temptation is to cut down the tree as I tried to do on Easter Sunday, 1975, when, believing the lie of Satan that I was doomed to a life of illness, blindness, and uselessness, I tried to kill myself. I, like the tree, was given another chance, and I'm all new. I've made a resurrection commitment to God to be a better person for His sake. I am asking Him to help me take my eyes off the introspective and focus on the outer perspective. I've committed myself to look at the opportunities and limitations of family, home, washing and clean-ing and even illness and see them as the sun, rain, and food that will grow me into what He designed me to be. I, like the tree, want to offer more shade and comfort to those who walk my way. I want to point them to the beauty rather than the ugliness. And if they are in the bare times in their life, I want to reassure them that it is temporary and resurrection may be right around the corner. What I want most of all to do is express the magnificence of being a woman in such a way that it will let others see their own magnificence. I do believe in the magnificence of women.

Don't be led astray by women who have lost the overall perspective of God's plan, who are looking more for significance than magnificence. Don't curse your soft curves and wish to be a man. You see, even man has his limitations. As much as he may dream, he can never receive the gift of life into his body, nurture it, give birth to it, and then have the God-ordained privilege of bringing it to maturity.

As I view my children approaching maturity, I can see, as through a glass, darkly, what God had in mind when he said I was to be a "keeper at home." I may not see the whole picture until eternity. I do see that I am to cease asking the Potter why He made me this way, and yield into His tender hands my very life. Mary said, "My soul doth magnify the Lord," when God revealed that her purpose was carrying and giving birth to God's own Son. Little did she know at that moment of her magnificence that she would watch Him die a cruel death on a cross. Was her life worth it? Now that she is forever with her Son and Savior in heaven, I'm sure she sees the whole plan.

Esther expressed her magnificence by declaring her willingness to die to save her people.

Will you express yours by sacrificing to spare your family?

Notes

CHAPTER 1

1. Caroline Bird, *The Two-Paycheck Marriage* (New York: Simon & Schuster, Pocket Books, 1979), inside cover page.
2. Ibid., p. 279.
3. Ibid., p. 286.
4. Ibid.
5. Edith Schaeffer, *What Is a Family?* (Old Tappan, NJ: Fleming H. Revell Co., 1975), p. 18.
6. Bird, *The Two-Paycheck Marriage*, p. 287.
7. Ibid.

CHAPTER 2

1. Dale Evans Rogers, *Hear the Children Crying* (Old Tappan, NJ: Fleming H. Revell Co., 1978), pp. 61–62.
2. Edith Schaeffer, *What Is a Family?*
3. James Dobson, *What Wives Wish Their Husbands Knew about Women* (Wheaton: Tyndale House, 1975), p. 58.
4. Bird, *The Two-Paycheck Marriage*, p. 37.
5. Quoted in Phyllis Schlafly, *The Power of the Positive Woman* (New York: Harcourt Brace Jovanovich, Jove Publications, 1977), p. 58.
6. Ibid., p. 57.

CHAPTER 3

1. *Webster's New World Dictionary* (Nashville: Southwestern Co., 1978), p. 410.
2. *American Jurisprudence*, 2d, vol. 41, "Husband and Wife," secs. 329–32, 334. Quoted in Schlafly, *The Power of the Positive Woman*, p. 89.
3. Schlafly, *The Power of the Positive Woman*, p. 99.
4. Lynda G. Parry, "Why Working Mothers Make Me Mad," *McCall's* magazine, February 1981.

CHAPTER 4

1. Bird, *The Two-Paycheck Marriage*, p. 296.
2. Beverly LaHaye, *I Am a Woman by God's Design* (Old Tappan, NJ: Fleming H. Revell Co., 1980), p. 94.

CHAPTER 5

1. *Book of Knowledge, s.v.*
2. Bird, *The Two-Paycheck Marriage*, pp. 297–98.
3. Larry Christenson, *The Christian Family* (Minneapolis: Bethany Fellowship, 1970), pp. 10–11.
4. Elisabeth Elliot, *Shadow of the Almighty* (Grand Rapids: Zondervan Publishing House, 1958), back cover.

CHAPTER 6

1. LaHaye, *I Am a Woman by God's Design*, p. 61.
2. Ibid., p. 60.
3. Dean Merrill, *The Husband Book* (Grand Rapids: Zondervan Publishing House, 1977), p. 133.
4. Bird, *The Two-Paycheck Marriage*, p. 79.
5. Ibid., p. 73.
6. Ibid., p. 104.
7. Ibid., p. 117.
8. Merrill, *The Husband Book*, p. 53.

CHAPTER 7

1. Elisabeth Elliot, *Let Me Be a Woman* (Wheaton: Tyndale House, 1976), p. 54.

2. *The Good Housekeeping Woman's Almanac* (New York: Newspaper Enterprise Association, 1977), p. 555.
3. *The Lynchburg (Virginia) Daily Advance*, November 1980.
4. *The Good Housekeeping Woman's Almanac*, p. 63.
5. Beverly LaHaye, *The Spirit-Controlled Woman* (Irvine, CA: Harvest House, 1976), p. 71.
6. Maxine Hancock, *Love, Honor—and Be Free* (Chicago: Moody Press, 1975), pp. 22–23.
7. Schlafly, *The Power of the Positive Woman*, p. 61.
8. Fourteenth Amendment; Higher Education Act of 1972; Comprehensive Health Manpower Training Act of 1971; Federal Equal Credit Opportunity Act of 1975; Comprehensive Employment and Training Act of 1973; quoted in LaHaye, *I Am a Woman by God's Design*, p. 132.
9. Hancock, *Love, Honor—and Be Free*, p. 27.
10. Quoted in Sally Wendkos Olds, "Do You Have What It Takes to Make a Good Marriage?", *Ladies Home Journal*, October 1980.
11. Hancock, *Love, Honor—and Be Free*, p. 34.
12. Elliot, *Let Me Be a Woman*, pp. 52–53.
13. LaHaye, *I Am a Woman by God's Design*, pp. 107–8.

Chapter 8

1. Rogers, *Hear the Children Crying*, p. 22.
2. Ibid., p. 23.
3. Ibid.
4. Ibid., p. 39.
5. Geraldine Carro, "Parents and Babies: How the Love Affair Beings," *Ladies Home Journal*, May 1981.
6. LaHaye, *I Am a Woman by God's Design*, p. 28.
7. Paul D. Meier and Linda Burnett, from p. 33 of *The Unwanted Generation*. Copyright 1980 by Baker Book House and used by permission.
8. Rogers, *Hear the Children Crying*, p. 109.
9. Meier and Burnett, *The Unwanted Generation*, p. 93.
10. Dobson, *What Wives Wish Their Husbands Knew about Women*, p. 56.
11. Joyce Godman, "Vacuum-packed Day Care," *Ms* magazine, March 1975, p. 50.
12. Meier and Burnett, *The Unwanted Generation*, p. 55.
13. Ibid.
14. LaHaye, *I Am a Woman by God's Design*, p. 105.
15. Ibid.

CHAPTER 9

1. Dean Merrill, *The Husband Book* (Grand Rapids: Zondervan Publishing House, 1977), p. 12.

CHAPTER 10

1. *Newsweek*, Sept. 1, 1980.
2. Quoted in *The Lynchburg (Virginia) Daily Advance*, May 6, 1981.
3. Ibid.
4. *Newsweek*, Sept. 1, 1980.
5. Ibid.
6. Ibid.
7. Ibid.
8. Tim and Beverly LaHaye, *The Act of Marriage* (Grand Rapids: Zondervan Publishing House, 1976), pp. 209, 210.
9. Elliot, *Let Me Be a Woman*, p. 36.
10. Ibid., p. 165.
11. Ibid., pp. 166, 167.

CHAPTER 11

1. Bird, *The Two-Paycheck Marriage*, pp. 167–68.
2. Maggie Scarf, *Unfinished Business: Pressure Points in the Lives of Women* (New York: Doubleday, 1980).